"*Supporting Neurodivergent and Autistic People for Their Transition into Adulthood: Blueprints for Education, Training, and Employment* is a MUST read. Through initial sharing of personal and lived experience, the author immediately creates a deeply human connection with the reader that goes far beyond blueprints. All of the concepts are framed with an appreciation and understanding of the importance of context, and individual goals and values. From the emphasis on developing the whole person, to educator roles, expectations, training, motivation, feedback, ethics, and more; this book delivers a framework with immense depth and scope. An excellent and thoroughly enlightening read."
  —**Dr. Amanda Kelly**, *President and CEO of Firefly Autism, Co-Founder of the Colorado Neurodiversity Chamber of Commerce*

"This book is a much needed guide to help those supporting developing young adults on the spectrum find meaning and purpose in adulthood. Based on his experience as the parent of an autistic young man, and his ongoing efforts to secure employment for autistic individuals within the trades, Danny has provided the blueprints for others to build a sustainable future. His insights into teaching, training, and job skill readiness are invaluable. Highly recommended."
  —**Dr. Tom Welsh**, *psychologist and author of* The Breakaway: A Parent's Guide to Transitioning the Autistic and Twice Exceptional Adolescent Into Young Adulthood

Supporting Neurodivergent and Autistic People for Their Transition into Adulthood

This trailblazing resource teaches educators how to support the strengths of children and teens on the autism spectrum as they transition into their lives as adults.

Offering ideas and solutions to counter the currently steep unemployment rate for those on the autism spectrum in the United States, each chapter takes a strength- and asset-based approach to autism and neurodivergent education, training, and employment. The author draws upon his lived experience as a parent to a neurodivergent child to provide unique and proven strategies with real-life applications.

Secondary and post-secondary educators can learn to refresh their current standards of practice and the concept of what is possible and appropriate in working with students on the autism spectrum.

Danny Combs has a master's degree in education and is a Board-Certified Cognitive Specialist and a Certified Autism Specialist. He was granted several awards in teaching – including a Grammy Enterprise Award for the program he designed in the Nashville schools – and became a published educational author, arranger, and songwriter and served as Board Chair/President of the Autism Society. He has two incredible children – Dylan and Ellie. When his son, Dylan, was diagnosed with autism, Danny formed Teaching the Autism Community Trades (TACT) with the mission to encourage and empower the full spectrum of individuals with autism through education and employment in the skilled trades.

Other Eye On Education Books Available from Routledge
(www.routledge.com/eyeoneducation)

Remote Learning Strategies for Students with IEPs
An Educator's Guidebook
Kathryn Welby

Radical Principals
A Blueprint for Long-Term Equity and Stability at School
Michael S. Gaskell

Supporting Your Child with Special Needs
50 Fundamental Tools for Families
Rachel R. Jorgensen

Empowering Students for the Future
Using the Right Questions to Teach the Value of Passion, Success, and Failure
Eric Yuhasz

The Student Motivation Handbook
50 Ways to Boost an Intrinsic Desire to Learn
Larry Ferlazzo

From Ghosts to Graduates
An Educator's Guide to Identifying and Reconnecting Disengaged Students
Emily Freeland

Supporting Neurodivergent and Autistic People for Their Transition into Adulthood

Blueprints for Education, Training, and Employment

Danny Combs

Taylor & Francis Group

NEW YORK AND LONDON

Designed cover image: Shutterstock

First published 2024
by Routledge
605 Third Avenue, New York, NY 10158

and by Routledge
4 Park Square, Milton Park, Abingdon, Oxon, OX14 4RN

Routledge is an imprint of the Taylor & Francis Group, an informa business

© 2024 Danny Combs

The right of Danny Combs to be identified as author of this work has been asserted in accordance with sections 77 and 78 of the Copyright, Designs and Patents Act 1988.

All rights reserved. No part of this book may be reprinted or reproduced or utilised in any form or by any electronic, mechanical, or other means, now known or hereafter invented, including photocopying and recording, or in any information storage or retrieval system, without permission in writing from the publishers.

Trademark notice: Product or corporate names may be trademarks or registered trademarks, and are used only for identification and explanation without intent to infringe.

Library of Congress Cataloging-in-Publication Data
Names: Combs, Danny, author.
Title: Supporting neurodivergent and autistic people for their transition into adulthood : blueprints for education, training, and employment / Danny Combs.
Description: New York, NY : Routledge, 2024. | Includes bibliographical references.
Identifiers: LCCN 2023025663 (print) | LCCN 2023025664 (ebook) | ISBN 9781032406152 (hardback) | ISBN 9781032394916 (paperback) | ISBN 9781003353959 (ebook)
Subjects: LCSH: Youth with autism spectrum disorders—Education—United States. | Youth with autism spectrum disorders—Employment—United States.
Classification: LCC LC4718 .C66 2024 (print) | LCC LC4718 (ebook) | DDC 371.940973—dc23/eng/20230825
LC record available at https://lccn.loc.gov/2023025663
LC ebook record available at https://lccn.loc.gov/2023025664

ISBN: 978-1-032-40615-2 (hbk)
ISBN: 978-1-032-39491-6 (pbk)
ISBN: 978-1-003-35395-9 (ebk)

DOI: 10.4324/9781003353959

Typeset in Palatino
by Apex CoVantage, LLC

Contents

Foreword ix

Introduction 1

SECTION 1
In the Classroom 5

1 Identifying Strength 7

2 Listening. 15

3 Setting Up Sequencing 21

4 Understanding the Difference Between Skill
   and Ability. 26

5 Holistic Approach. 30

6 Demeanor of Educator. 33

7 Assessment 37

8 Deception Without Deceit 58

SECTION 2
Training. 63

9 Simulation Site 65

10 Failure to Succeed. 69

11 Holistic Approach..................................72

12 Slow to Go Fast..77

13 Setup of Training....................................83

14 Assessment 95

15 Feedback..99

SECTION 3
Placement **103**

16 Portfolio 105

17 Work-Based Interview..............................113

18 Talent Over Charity.................................119

19 Employer Communication 121

20 Assimilation vs Integration 124

21 Job Coaching..126

22 Parent Expectations 129

23 Benefits..132

Conclusion/Final Thoughts   135
Bibliography   140

Foreword

This is a book that I've wanted to write for a long time. I'm so grateful I had the chance and opportunity. My son Dylan inspired me and changed my world. All of my kids have. I hope it serves all parents, educators, and individuals to see that neurodiversity is beautiful. Autism is not something that needs to be cured or changed but rather has inspiring and wonderful qualities. My son has a future. Thank you for reading, and I hope you enjoy it.

Introduction

My world was forever changed on January 8th, 2009. At this point in my timeline, I was in Nashville working as a professional musician and educator. After finishing my bachelor's degree in music in 2003, I was one of the lucky ones that scored a job in the music industry. In fact, even before graduating, I drove down early for a meeting at ASCAP (the American Society of Composers and Publishers) as they wanted to listen to my music and become my performing rights organization. I remember sitting in a terrible bar on Music Row at 1 a.m. drinking a God-awful light beer thinking, "Wow, I can't believe this is working out!" And work out it did. I spent those first few years working with artists in a variety of forms – studio work, performance, management, publicity, publishing, arranging, and teaching.

Life was good. And on January 8th, 2009, it got even better. My son was born. This ten-pound bundle of pure joy came screaming into the world with purpose. I was captured completely by him. The only song I've ever written in one take was sitting by his crib and watching him sleep. He was and is my boy.

A couple of years into his life, we started noticing some unique and distinctive attributes that didn't seem to align with our friends' kids of a similar age. At the time, all our friends were posting on Facebook these images of how great their child was and bragging about all their developmental milestones. Dylan just wasn't there yet. We took him to the doctor, who encouraged us to see another doctor, who encouraged us to see another doctor, and on and on it went. We finally came to learn Dylan had autism.

Those words rocked me to my core. I literally made the person that told me cry. Even though, at the time, I didn't even know the stats about it, I knew "it wasn't good." According to the CDC in 2022, 1 in 44 eight-year-old children is diagnosed with autism. That's a lot. A whole lot. And my son Dylan is one of them.

I admit that I had selfish, terrible thoughts about what that meant to *me*. I thought I wouldn't have grandkids. My family name wouldn't carry on. That he'd live in my basement or end up in a group home. Selfish, selfish, selfish. But honest.

I was not going to let this diagnosis beat him, or me. I decided to dive in and learn more. I learned about the educational models used, the behavioral approach accepted, the unbelievable 90% un(der)employment rate – which is the highest of ANY demographic – and the overall complete lack of resources for parents once they hit the transition age and adulthood. Now, at the time, my boy was young. But I was scared.

Some people may tell you I'm stubborn. Some may just say determined. But either way, most would agree I would make sure my son had a future and didn't become a number.

During my time in Nashville, I went back to school and earned my master's degree from Lipscomb University in teaching music. I loved all the educational theories, practices, and history. I immersed myself in it. And you know what? I was good at it. I had great professors that really inspired me. I found myself being quite progressive and looking at the standard quota with complete disdain. I went to an inner-city school and developed a very successful music program. In fact, it won a Grammy. I wrote the curriculum that Nashville public schools adopted, had some educational articles published, and was successful with my ideas and practices.

As I watched my son, I noticed something I wasn't hearing from any of these therapists. He had strengths. Lots of strengths. But the therapists didn't see it. They saw autism and weakness. Now, that's not to put them down. They truly helped change his life but missed major portions of it at the same time. He could build things – could seemingly visualize, conceptualize, and then make incredible 3D things. This was all before he could even say, "Hello, Dad."

My family background was in the skilled trades, so I could tell he was good. Really good. So, I started looking around for a strengths-based program that used the skilled trades to provide a holistic educational model that leans toward employment and a better future.

I couldn't find one.

I ended up meeting an incredible individual named Dr. Temple Grandin. I told her about my ideas, and she told me to do it. So, I put down my guitar and did it. It's called TACT, which stands for Teaching the Autism Community Trades. The ideas, practices, and methods we use have led to a near 180-degree turnaround in the employment rate and a future model that is working. Right now, Children's Hospital is doing a three-year study on its outcomes and outputs. I can't wait to share them. And Dr. Grandin – I now consider her a dear friend.

In this book, I want to share with you a possibility that hasn't been developed. Food for thought that can help perhaps guide your classroom – create inclusion, create results that you haven't seen. And perhaps, if we're lucky, your students, or your child, will find themselves and a future that wouldn't have been possible. That's the goal. Maybe we can show the world just how overlooked and disenfranchised this group is. And they shouldn't be. They're incredible, and they deserve the same future as anyone. Let's build it together. Let's build with TACT and begin.

1
In the Classroom

1

Identifying Strength

The starting point in the blueprints for autism is strength. Simple, right? Gosh, I wish that were true. If you're an experienced autism educator, it may be even harder. That isn't because you don't see strengths or believe in them but because the entire setup for an autistic individual is deficit-based. That's not our model. And, thus, a keystone in our approach is identifying and then building upon strengths. By and large, most autism educational models, practices, and theories are based upon deficiency – the exact opposite of what I'm suggesting. They look at a student as an individual with problems that need to be fixed, adjusted, modified, punished, or assimilated.

I'm not suggesting that at all. I suggest you look at what they're good at *first*, start there, and build from that.

Every individual has something they're good at. Either natural or learned. Likewise, they have interests, dislikes, and tendencies. However, as educators, especially classroom educators, we're put in a terrible position of somehow molding each student through a curriculum or pathway that is imposed upon us. And molding should not be the goal. That gives us little room for finding strengths. Especially in the timeframes provided too. And, in large class size numbers, like 35 to 50 students in a class, that is darn near impossible. It's a losing situation for everyone involved. It's easy to see the weakness rather than the possibility.

Assessing and discovering an individual's emotional, creative, cognitive, and social strengths is an important aspect of

DOI: 10.4324/9781003353959-3

understanding their overall well-being and potential for growth and development. It is difficult but paramount. After all, we're building towards the future for each individual.

I want to start right away with a story; stories are so important. As this book progresses, we'll dive more into the lingo used daily as employers or educators, so let me please start as a dad. The story is of a young man who came to one of our very first classes. This was when I was driving around in a 1958 Chevy panel truck going door to door. We were restoring a 1975 Jeep Cherokee out of a donor's garage. It was once owned by a firefighter, and, ironically, the engine had caught on fire. We were going to pull the engine, rebuild it (if we could), and restore the car. Let's call this young man Paul. Paul was kicked out of his high school auto class because of his "behavior." His teachers only saw that, and he was lost. He didn't believe in himself but knew he loved cars.

When he came to our first class, we saw this strength and let him know it. We built him up and supported his strengths. As time went by, he became a better and better mechanic and got back into his high school auto program. When he graduated, he was ranked third in his class. Isn't that amazing? He let his talent speak and carry his voice, and thankfully, his teacher listened and recognized it. He succeeded. We were so proud.

These strengths also play a vital role in an individual's mental and emotional well-being, their ability to form and maintain relationships, and their ability to navigate and succeed in the world around them. Understanding and building on these strengths can help individuals to live happier, more fulfilling lives and to achieve their goals and aspirations.

There are lots of established tests educators utilize. Emotional strength is often assessed through self-reported measures such as surveys or questionnaires. These measures typically assess individuals' emotional regulation, resilience, and overall emotional well-being. Some common measures of emotional strength include the Emotional Intelligence Scale, the Emotional Resilience Scale, and the Mental Health Continuum Scale. These measures can provide valuable information about an individual's emotional strengths and areas for improvement. For example, the Emotional Intelligence Scale measures an individual's ability to perceive, understand, and manage their own emotions and the emotions of others. The Emotional Resilience Scale measures an individual's ability to cope with stress and bounce back from adversity. These measures can provide insight into an individual's emotional strengths and areas where they may need to develop better emotional regulation and resilience.

Creative strength is often assessed through tasks or activities that measure an individual's ability to generate new and original ideas, solve problems, and think outside the box. Some common measures of creative strength include the Torrance Test of Creative Thinking, the Abbreviated Torrance Test for Adults, and the Creative Problem Solving Assessment. These measures can provide valuable information about an individual's creative strengths and areas for improvement. For example, the Torrance Test of Creative Thinking measures an individual's ability to generate new ideas and think creatively in various contexts. The Creative Problem Solving Assessment measures an individual's ability to identify problems, generate possible solutions, and evaluate the effectiveness of different solutions. These measures can provide insight into an individual's creative strengths and areas where they may need to develop their problem-solving and critical-thinking skills.

Cognitive strength is often assessed through tests and measures that evaluate an individual's intelligence, memory, attention, and other cognitive abilities. Some common measures of cognitive strength include the Wechsler Adult Intelligence Scale, the Woodcock-Johnson Tests of Cognitive Abilities, and the Digit Span Test. The Vineland is also used a lot in the autism community for executive functioning. These measures can provide valuable information about an individual's cognitive strengths. For example, the Wechsler Adult Intelligence Scale measures an individual's overall intelligence and can provide information about their verbal comprehension, perceptual reasoning, working memory, and processing speed. The Woodcock-Johnson Tests of Cognitive Abilities measures an individual's cognitive abilities in specific areas such as reading, math, and written language. The Digit Span Test measures an individual's working memory and attention span. These measures can provide insight into an individual's cognitive strengths and areas where they may need to develop their memory, attention, and cognitive abilities. However, please keep in mind the methods by which these tests are administered are usually geared towards neurotypicals and may pose a challenge to the neurodiverse community.

Diving deeper, social strength is often assessed through self-reported measures such as surveys or questionnaires. These measures typically assess an individual's ability to form and maintain healthy relationships, communicate effectively, and navigate social situations. Some common measures of social strength include the Interpersonal Competence Scale, the Social Support Questionnaire, and the Social Skills Inventory. These measures can provide valuable information about an individual's social strengths and areas for improvement. For example, the Interpersonal Competence Scale measures an individual's ability to form and maintain healthy relationships, while the Social Support Questionnaire measures an individual's perceived level of social support.

The Social Skills Inventory measures an individual's ability to communicate on a neurotypical scale while listening actively and navigating social situations. These measures can provide insight into how a test measures an individual's ability to form and maintain healthy relationships, communicate, and navigate social situations. The Social Support Questionnaire measures an individual's level of social support and sense of belonging. The Social Skills Inventory measures an individual's ability to understand and navigate social cues, express emotions, and engage in appropriate social behaviors. These measures can provide insight into an individual's social strengths and areas where they may need to develop their social skills and relationships.

It's also important to note that assessing and discovering one's emotional, creative, cognitive, and social strengths should not be done in isolation but rather in context and in relation to one's values and goals. For example, an individual who values independence and self-expression may have a high level of emotional and creative strengths but may not prioritize social or cognitive strengths as much, and that's totally fine. Additionally, the assessment results should be used as a tool for self-discovery and personal growth and should be discussed with a professional who can provide guidance and support.

Furthermore, it's important to note that these methods of assessment have their own benefits and limitations. Self-reported measures, while quick and easy to administer, may be prone to bias, while tests and activities are more objective but may not fully capture the complexity of the traits being assessed. Additionally, it's important to use multiple methods and sources of information when assessing an individual's strengths, as this can provide a more comprehensive understanding of their abilities. For example, an individual may score highly on a creativity test, but it's important to also consider their real-life experiences and accomplishments in order to get a more complete picture of their creative strengths.

Assessing and discovering an individual's emotional, creative, cognitive, and social strengths is an important aspect of understanding their overall well-being and potential for growth and development. There are many different methods for assessing these strengths, including self-reported measures, tasks, activities, and cognitive tests. It is important to use multiple methods and sources of information when assessing an individual's strengths, as this can provide a more comprehensive understanding of their abilities. Furthermore, it's important to assess these strengths in context and in relation to an individual's values and goals and to use the results as a tool for self-discovery and personal growth rather than as a label or a limitation.

But of all those fancy tests, I'm a big fan of something simpler: formative assessment through customization and differentiation. This takes time, though, as it requires attention and participation from each and every student. And in this case, I'm going to make the argument that, at the start of a relationship with a new student or client, you take the time. Starting slowly with each student, gauging the things they are naturally good at, can be so impactful. While some classrooms are divided by "how affected" someone on the spectrum is, I find that the formative approach works with everyone, neurodiverse or neurotypical individuals alike.

Some of the key points I like to look for are subtle but important. Let's start with the subtle observation of expression through body language. Your ability to perceive and pick up on these reactions during the assessment is paramount.

Compound that with some external influences (which we'll discuss later), and you have a good starting place look by assessing

- Joy
- Happiness
- Smilies
- Questions/Response
- Grit
- Sticking with it
- Attention
- Curiosity
- Aggravation
- Frustration Tolerance
- Executive Functioning
- Spatial Awareness
- Background
- Parent Influence

What comes to mind when you see this list? Does it seem simple, generic, or perhaps even difficult? If you have a hundred students, are you able to start with something like this for each and every one? But this is where I like to start, over all those models mentioned earlier. A model that came out of Dartmouth in the '80s called IPS or Individual Placement and Support talks about how a working professional should never have more than 20 clients – tops. The research found it becomes nearly impossible to truly address a list like the one mentioned earlier if there is a higher student-to-teacher ratio than that. That's super ahead of its time. I would argue that six students per class is the maximum and agree with no more than 20 clients per teacher or case manager. Sadly, most of us will not get that luxury.

Let's break down this list. The first three items are all about excitement. Right off the bat, we're looking for what makes the student or client happy. We do this because, if we can discover an interest, it may be associated with strength. We're observing for a spark, even the hint of one. Remember, most autism programs are deficit-based, and young individuals are conditioned and trained to respond rather than jump with excitement. So, it's going to start small, but it will be there. And as we move down the list, we're looking for how hard a student is willing to work, intrinsically.

Behaviorists look for external motivators because they're looking for weaknesses first and then what prize can win them over. While that does have its place, it's not what we're suggesting as a starting point.

In order to administer some foundational formative assessment, you'll need to set up a project or two. I love project-based learning, and a fun project in any subject that's hands-on is an amazing place to start. And when you set up the first assessment to gauge the previously mentioned list, the project should be designed for them to succeed while also looking for their zone of proximal development. It's your job to give them that, but it's not a freebie token participation trophy. They have to earn the win, but the assessment is designed to lead them there. They need a win from the start. I like to call it "deception without deceit" – the illusion that, during the project, they're in control, but actually, they're demonstrating what you're assessing for.

How do you help lead them there or gently push them towards it? For that, we must discuss the importance of questioning.

The right questions are not easy, especially when some institutions ask educators to annotate all their questions in their lesson plans. That's restricting and doesn't leave room for adaptation or modification. Make no mistake, good assessment comes with good adaptation. However, the key to discovering those strengths is questions. The right questions.

I always recommend starting with Socratic questioning. It's a dialog and engagement rather than a pedagogically led discussion. You need to earn the student or client's trust, and, by engaging in genuine, heartfelt dialog, you can do that. You must remain andragogical in your approach and keep the client first.

That, in combination with a positive lead compliment based on your formative assessment, can be a winning ticket.

While I find those types of questions are difficult to blankly narrate, it may be something along the lines of "Timmy, the way you naturally kept your left hand on the board while away from the saw was really smart. How did you learn that? And do you see how amazing the cut was? You did that without any of my help! Did that make sense?"

You're probing for rationale and reasoning, which can help you fine-tune your assessment and lead you toward their strength.

2
Listening

At the core of learning is listening. A lot of people might not agree with that, but I've found it to be so foundational. There are so many different types of listening, and so few people understand them all and especially their role in learning. It always breaks my heart when I see teachers, researchers, and instructors speaking without listening. Do you see that I'm talking about with the educator/administration/parent not listening? Not the individual with autism. And if the person leading isn't listening, is it really about the student at that point? How then can we set up sequencing, lessons, or goals without listening? But this is not just on the teacher front but on the student front too. So, we must model it and teach it.

Let's start by identifying a few types of listening:

- Hearing: the automatic, passive process of registering noises or sounds.
- Listening: the semi-conscious selective filtering of sounds to engage (some) thinking.
- Listening *For*: the conscious act of anticipating and focusing on specific sounds or ideas.
- Active Listening: the conscious act of attempting to understand the total message, complete with nuances, nonverbal communication, the use of clarifying questions, etc.
- Empathetic Listening: active listening from another person's perspective.

These are important to reiterate because, as you question your students, you must make sure you're aware of how you're listening and how it goes hand and hand with questioning. Teachers and leaders are role models of listening. So much can be learned about a client – their passion, their goals – bringing it back to the beginning: identifying their strength.

Again, as a teacher, asking good questions is essential to engaging students, promoting critical thinking, and assessing their understanding of the subject matter. However, asking good questions requires more than just the ability to frame questions correctly. It also requires the ability to listen actively and attentively to the students' responses. In this chapter and section, I'm hoping we can dive deeper into how listening is important for teachers to ask good questions of their students and how it can help to create a positive and effective learning environment.

Active listening is a crucial component of effective teaching. When teachers listen attentively to their students, they can better understand their learning needs, assess their progress, and provide feedback that is tailored to their individual needs. Additionally, active listening can help teachers to build positive relationships with their students, which can lead to a more productive and supportive learning environment.

One of the primary benefits of listening in teaching is that it can help teachers to identify the strengths and weaknesses of their students. By listening carefully to their responses, teachers can gain insight into students' thought processes, identify any misconceptions, and tailor their teaching approach to address these issues. For example, if a student struggles to understand a concept, the teacher can use active listening to identify where the student is having difficulty and provide targeted feedback and support.

Active listening can also help teachers to assess the effectiveness of their teaching strategies. By listening to their students' feedback and responses, teachers can gain insight into what works and what doesn't and adjust their teaching approach accordingly. This can lead to more effective teaching strategies and better outcomes for students.

Additionally, active listening can help to build trust and rapport between teachers and students. When teachers listen to their students with genuine interest and attention, they signal that they care about their students' thoughts, feelings, and perspectives. This can lead to greater engagement and participation from students and a more positive and supportive learning environment.

Asking good questions is essential to effective teaching. Good questions can promote critical thinking, encourage students to articulate their thoughts and ideas, and help teachers assess their understanding of the subject matter. However, asking good questions requires more than just the ability to frame questions correctly. It also requires the ability to listen attentively to the students' responses and use that information to guide further inquiry.

Good questions are open-ended and encourage students to think deeply about the subject matter. They also require students to explain their thinking and provide evidence to support their claims. Additionally, good questions should be tailored to the students' level of understanding and encourage them to build on their existing knowledge.

Active listening is essential for asking good questions of students. When teachers listen attentively to their students' responses, they can use that information to guide further inquiry and promote critical thinking. Additionally, active listening can help teachers to identify any misconceptions or gaps in understanding that need to be addressed.

One strategy for active listening is to use reflective listening. Reflective listening involves paraphrasing and summarizing the students' responses to ensure that the teacher has understood them correctly. This can help to clarify any misunderstandings and encourage students to elaborate on their ideas. Additionally, reflective listening can help to build trust and rapport with students by demonstrating that the teacher is genuinely interested in their thoughts and ideas.

Another strategy for active listening is to use probing questions. Probing questions are designed to encourage students to think more deeply about the subject matter and provide evidence to support their claims. For example, if a student provides a simple response to a question, the teacher can use probing questions to encourage the student to explain their thinking in more detail.

Active listening can also help teachers to identify any biases or assumptions that may be influencing their questioning. By listening attentively to their students' responses, teachers can identify any gaps in their own knowledge and understanding, which can then inform their questioning and guide further inquiry. Additionally, active listening can help teachers to remain open-minded and nonjudgmental, which can create a safe and supportive learning environment where students feel comfortable sharing their thoughts and ideas.

Active listening can also help teachers to tailor their questioning to the individual needs and abilities of their students. For example, if a student is struggling to understand a concept, the teacher can use active listening to identify where the student is having difficulty and provide targeted feedback and support. Alternatively, if a student demonstrates a deep understanding of a subject, the teacher can use active listening to encourage them to explore the topic further and develop their thinking.

Furthermore, active listening can help teachers to model good questioning skills for their students. By listening attentively to their students' responses and asking follow-up questions, teachers can demonstrate how to ask good questions and encourage their students to develop these skills themselves. This can lead to a more engaging and collaborative learning environment, where students feel empowered to ask questions and explore the subject matter in greater depth.

And what goes hand-in-hand with that is good questioning.

Some Suggestions for Good Qualitative and Quantitative Questions

It's Not About You
We know the world is telling you the exact opposite, but if you're going to be a good listener for your students, you must never forget this fact.

Empathy vs Passive Aggression

It may seem like we're splitting hairs here, but the devil is in the details, and a fundamental part of good questioning and listening is genuine empathy. A lot of educators, and people in general, are incredibly passive-aggressive. This goes back to our first point; they confuse these two because they are making it about themselves. Please don't make it about you! Remember, listen with the heart.

Kindness Isn't Weakness

When a teacher is engaged in questioning and active listening with their students, co-workers, or parents, it's important that they use kindness in their demeanor. The affective part of listening cannot be understood. Your students must trust you to open up, and you'll be able to ask better questions, learn more about them, and, thus, ask more questions.

Remember Humility

This is the bookend to remembering it's not about you. Pride will get in the way of good listening. Keep a memory or experience in the back of your mind.

Asking good questions is a key aspect of effective teaching, as it can help to engage students and promote critical thinking. Good questions can also help to create a classroom environment that is conducive to learning and discovery. In this section, we will discuss several strategies for asking students good questions.

One strategy for asking good questions is to use open-ended questions. Open-ended questions are questions that cannot be answered with a simple yes or no. They require students to think critically and provide a more detailed response. For example, instead of asking, "Did you understand the material?" an open-ended question could be "What did you find most challenging about the material?" Open-ended questions encourage students to think critically and provide more detailed responses.

Another strategy for asking good questions is to use probing questions. Probing questions are used to follow up on a student's response and encourage them to provide more detail or to think more deeply about the topic. For example, after a student has provided a response, a probing question could be "Can you give an example?" or "What led you to that conclusion?" Probing questions encourage students to think more deeply and critically about the topic and can help to uncover misconceptions or misunderstandings.

A third strategy for asking good questions is to use questions that promote higher-order thinking skills. Higher-order thinking skills include analysis, synthesis, and evaluation. These types of questions require students to think critically, make connections, and evaluate information. For example, instead of asking, "What did you learn?" a higher-order thinking question could be "What connections can you make between this material and what we have learned previously?" or "How do you evaluate the credibility of the sources we have used?" Higher-order thinking questions encourage students to think critically, make connections, and evaluate information, which can help deepen their understanding of the material.

It is important to note that asking good questions is not just about the question itself but also the timing and the context in which it is asked. Asking good questions at the right time, in the right context, and with the right tone can help to create an environment that is conducive to learning and discovery. Additionally, it's important to listen carefully to the student's responses and to follow up with probing questions when necessary to encourage deeper thinking and understanding.

As we set up good listening practices and move those into questioning, it'll help you set up sequencing, which is going to play a pivotal role in the transition, especially the transition into employment.

3

Setting Up Sequencing

Sequencing for autism education refers to the process of breaking down complex tasks or information into smaller, manageable steps in order to help individuals with autism understand and complete them. This can include activities such as daily routines, social interactions, and academic tasks. Sometimes, you hear this called "scaffolding," but either way, and no matter how you choose to talk about it, it's important.

The first step in setting up sequencing for autism education is to identify the specific task or information that needs to be broken down. This may involve working with the individual with autism, as well as their parents or caregivers, to understand their needs and abilities. Next, the task or information should be broken down into smaller, manageable steps. These steps should be clearly defined and written down so that they can be easily understood and followed by the individual with autism. It's important to make sure the steps are simple, concrete, and logical.

It is also important to include visual aids such as pictures or diagrams to help the individual understand the steps. Dr. Temple Grandin will be the first to tell you the value of visual thinking for autistic education. I agree. Visual aids can be especially helpful for individuals with autism who may have difficulty understanding verbal instructions.

Once the steps have been defined and written down, they should be reviewed and practiced with the individual with autism. This can be done through role-playing, repetition, and feedback. It is important to be patient, flexible, and positive while providing the support and guidance needed for the individual to successfully complete the task.

It's also important to provide the individual with autism with feedback and positive reinforcement for their progress. This can help to build their confidence and encourage them to continue working on the task.

It's important to regularly review and update the steps as needed. As the individual with autism progresses, the steps may need to be modified or adjusted to reflect their increased abilities and understanding. Setting up sequencing for autism education involves identifying the task or information that needs to be broken down, breaking it down into smaller, manageable steps, providing visual aids, reviewing and practicing the steps with the individual with autism, providing feedback and positive reinforcement, and regularly reviewing and updating the steps as needed. It's a process that requires patience, flexibility, and a positive attitude, but with the right approach, it can be an effective way to help individuals with autism understand and complete complex tasks and information.

One of the key benefits of good strengths-based sequencing for a neuro-distinct individual is increased engagement. When individuals are given the opportunity to work on tasks and projects that align with their strengths, they are more likely to be motivated and engaged in the learning process. This is because they are able to see the relevance and value of the material and are able to apply their strengths to the task at hand. Additionally, when students feel confident in their abilities, they are more likely to take risks and be willing to try new things, which can lead to increased engagement and motivation.

Another benefit of good strengths-based sequencing is increased motivation. When students are able to utilize their strengths, they are more likely to feel a sense of accomplishment and pride in their work. This can lead to increased motivation and a desire to continue learning and growing. Additionally, when students feel that they are making progress and achieving success in areas that are important to them, they are more likely to be motivated to continue working toward and achieving their goals. And, sadly, a lot of time, individuals with autism rarely hear about or get to explore their strengths.

Again, good strengths-based sequencing also leads to increased overall success. When students are given the opportunity to work on tasks and projects that align with their strengths, they are more likely to be successful. This is because they are able to apply their natural talents and abilities to the task at hand, which increases the likelihood of success. Additionally, when students feel that they are making progress and achieving success, they are more likely to be motivated to continue working and achieving their goals.

It's important to note that good strengths-based sequencing is not just about identifying and utilizing the student's strengths but also providing opportunities for them to develop new skills and to learn to work on their areas of improvement. A well-rounded education should balance the development of strengths. This includes social skills and technical skills integrated holistically to identify their own areas of improvement. A holistic education should balance the development of strengths with the development of new skills and addressing areas of improvement. This is the zone of proximal development. This can be achieved by incorporating activities and tasks that challenge students in different ways and by providing opportunities for them to work on their areas of improvement while also building on their strengths.

One way to achieve this balance is through the use of differentiated instruction. Differentiated instruction is an approach to teaching that takes into account the diverse needs, abilities, and interests of students. It involves providing multiple paths to learning and assessing student understanding so that students can learn at their own pace and in a way that is most meaningful to them. This approach allows for the development of new skills and for addressing areas of improvement while also building on strengths.

Another way to achieve this balance is through the use of project-based learning. Project-based learning is an approach to teaching that involves students working on real-world projects that are relevant to their interests and passions. This approach allows students to apply their strengths and interests to the task at hand while also developing new skills and addressing areas of improvement. Additionally, it provides opportunities for students to work in teams, which can help them to learn how to collaborate and communicate effectively.

It's also important to consider the role of formative assessment in good strengths-based educational sequencing. Formative assessment is an ongoing process of gathering information about student understanding and progress throughout the learning process and using that information to adjust instruction and support student learning. Through the use of formative assessment, educators can gather information about student strengths and areas of improvement, which can inform their instruction and help ensure that the learning experiences align with the needs and abilities of their students.

In addition, it's important to involve students in the process of identifying their strengths and areas of improvement and to provide them with opportunities to reflect on their own learning. Self-reflection can help students to understand their own strengths and areas of improvement and to set goals for their own learning. Additionally, when students are involved in the process of identifying their strengths and areas of improvement, they are more likely to be invested in their own learning and take ownership of their own progress.

Good strengths-based educational sequencing is a vital aspect of effective education. It involves building on an individual's existing strengths and abilities while also providing opportunities for the development of new skills and for addressing areas of improvement. This approach to education leads to increased student engagement, motivation, and overall success. Good strengths-based educational sequencing can be achieved through the use of differentiated instruction, project-based learning, formative assessment, and involving students in the process of identifying their strengths and areas of improvement. It's important to remember that a well-rounded education should balance the development of strengths with the development of new skills and addressing areas of improvement in order to provide students with the best opportunities for growth and success. By incorporating good strengths-based educational sequencing into the curriculum and instruction, educators can help to create a classroom environment that is conducive to learning and discovery and to support student success.

4

Understanding the Difference Between Skill and Ability

I believe in the power of storytelling. The terms "skills" and "abilities" are often used interchangeably, but they refer to different aspects of a person's capabilities. People confuse these two. All the time. Let's look at a story to set the tone.

Once upon a time, there was a young man named Alex who loved woodworking. He had always been fascinated by the beauty of handmade wooden furniture and dreamed of becoming a skilled woodworker himself. Alex had a natural ability to work with wood. He could easily visualize the end product and had a good sense of how to shape and carve the wood to achieve his desired results. He was able to make basic pieces of furniture like tables and chairs without much effort.

One day, Alex decided to enter a woodworking competition. He felt confident in his ability and thought he would do well. However, when he arrived at the competition, he realized that he was not the only talented woodworker there. There were many other participants who had similar abilities to him. As the competition progressed, Alex started to realize that skill was more than just natural ability. He saw that the other woodworkers had spent years honing their craft and had developed a deep understanding of the materials and techniques used in woodworking.

Alex struggled to keep up with the other participants. His lack of skill showed as he made mistakes and struggled to achieve the precision and attention to detail that the other woodworkers displayed. In the end, Alex did not win the competition. However, he learned an important lesson about the difference between ability and skill. He realized that, while ability can be a great advantage, it is not enough to achieve excellence in woodworking. Skill is something that is developed over time through practice, experimentation, and learning from mistakes.

From that day on, Alex dedicated himself to improving his woodworking skills. He studied the techniques of other woodworkers, practiced relentlessly, and worked to refine his craftsmanship. Over time, his skill improved, and he became a highly respected and sought-after woodworker in his community.

This story shows that, while natural ability is helpful, skill is something that is earned through hard work and dedication. Alex was able to overcome his limitations and become an excellent woodworker by recognizing the importance of skill and committing himself to developing it.

Skills are learned abilities that are acquired through training, education, or practice, while abilities are innate talents or aptitudes that a person is born with. Both skills and abilities are important for personal and professional development, and they can interact and influence each other.

Skills refer to the ability to perform a specific task or activity. They are typically acquired through training, education, or practice and can be improved over time with additional experience. Skills can be divided into two categories: technical skills and soft skills. Technical skills refer to the ability to perform specific tasks, such as typing, cooking, playing a musical instrument, or programming a computer. Soft skills, on the other hand, refer to the ability to interact with others, such as communication, teamwork, and leadership.

The acquisition of skills is a process that occurs through different stages, including attention, retention, motor reproduction, and feedback. Attention refers to the ability to focus on a task, retention refers to the ability to remember the task, motor reproduction refers to the ability to perform the task, and feedback refers to the ability to adjust the task based on the results.

To acquire a new skill, a person must go through these stages, which can be influenced by various factors, such as motivation, interest, and the environment.

Skills can be improved and developed through practice and hard work. The more a person practices a skill, the more proficient they become at it. Additionally, skills can also be developed through education and training, which provide the necessary knowledge and resources to perform a task. For example, a person can learn how to cook by taking a cooking class or reading a cookbook, but they will only become a good cook through practice and experience.

Ability, on the other hand, refers to an innate or natural talent or aptitude for a particular task or activity. Abilities are generally considered to be inherent traits that a person is born with and cannot be easily acquired through training or education. Examples of abilities include intelligence, creativity, or athletic ability. These abilities are often considered to be the foundation for the development of skills. For example, a person with a natural aptitude for music may have an easier time learning to play a musical instrument than someone without that aptitude, but the person with the aptitude still needs to practice and develop the skill to become a proficient musician.

Abilities can be divided into two categories: cognitive abilities and physical abilities. Cognitive abilities refer to the mental abilities, such as intelligence, memory, and perception, while physical abilities refer to the abilities related to the body, such as strength, endurance, and coordination. These abilities can be measured through various tests and assessments, such as IQ tests, aptitude tests, and physical fitness tests.

It is important to note that skills and abilities are not mutually exclusive and can interact with each other. For example, a person with a natural aptitude for mathematics may have an easier time learning and developing mathematical skills than someone without that aptitude, but the person with the aptitude still needs to practice and develop the skills to excel in the subject.

Additionally, abilities can be developed and improved through practice and hard work, just like skills. For example, a person may not have a natural talent for athletics, but, through dedicated training and practice, they can improve their physical abilities and excel in sports.

Skills and abilities are different but complementary aspects of a person's capabilities. Skills are learned abilities that are acquired through training, education, or practice, while abilities are innate talents or aptitudes that a person is born with. Both skills and abilities are important for personal and professional development, and they can interact and influence each other. It is important to recognize the difference between the two in order to understand how they can be developed and improved and to make the most of one's capabilities. While abilities may provide a foundation for the development of skills, it is through practice and hard work that both skills and abilities can be honed and perfected. Thus, it is essential to always strive to improve both skills and abilities in order to achieve personal and professional success.

On a personal note, I want to add something that comes up a lot for some reason. Obviously, we view the autism spectrum as just that – a spectrum. To me, it should be viewed in a round, non-linear way. All individuals have strengths and abilities. Everyone. And when taking the time to really understand and support everyone, we can help them discover the path to the future.

5

Holistic Approach

Different models in education approach this uniquely, but at its core, holistic education is an approach to teaching and learning that focuses on the whole person, including their physical, emotional, intellectual, and spiritual well-being. It emphasizes the importance of developing the whole person rather than just focusing on academic achievement. This approach to education has been gaining popularity in recent years, as it recognizes that education is not just about preparing students for their future careers but also about helping them to lead fulfilling and well-rounded lives.

One of the main benefits of holistic education is that it helps to develop well-rounded individuals. By focusing on the whole person rather than just academic achievement, holistic education encourages students to develop a wide range of skills and interests. This can include developing physical fitness, creativity, emotional intelligence, and spiritual awareness. For example, students who have the opportunity to participate in physical education classes, sports teams, or other physical activities are more likely to maintain a healthy lifestyle and to have better physical health. Additionally, students who have the opportunity to participate in art, music, or drama classes are more likely to develop their creativity, which can be beneficial for their mental and emotional well-being.

Another benefit of holistic education is that it helps to foster a love of learning. When they receive a wide range of learning opportunities, students are more likely to find subjects and activities that they are passionate about. This can lead to increased engagement and motivation in their learning, which can ultimately lead to better academic outcomes. Additionally, when students are passionate about a subject, they are more likely to pursue it in the future, whether it be in college or as a career. This can lead to a lifetime of learning and personal growth.

Additionally, holistic education can help to develop critical-thinking skills. By exposing students to a wide range of subjects and perspectives, it encourages them to think critically and to consider different points of view. This can help students to develop their problem-solving and decision-making skills, which are essential for success in both their academic and professional lives. Furthermore, it also helps students to develop their ability to think independently and to question assumptions and beliefs, which can be particularly important in today's rapidly changing world.

Furthermore, holistic education can also lead to improved social and emotional well-being. By providing opportunities for students to develop their emotional intelligence and to learn about different cultures and perspectives, holistic education better prepares them to navigate the complexities of the world. This can lead to increased empathy, understanding, and respect for others, which can ultimately lead to a more peaceful and just society. Additionally, holistic education can also help students to develop their self-awareness, self-esteem, and self-confidence, which are essential for their personal and social development.

Holistic education also encourages students to take an active role in their own learning. When provided with opportunities to set their own goals, make decisions, and take responsibility for their learning, students are more likely to be motivated and engaged in the learning process. This is particularly important as it prepares students for life beyond school and helps to foster a sense of self-awareness, self-motivation, and self-esteem. Furthermore, by taking an active role in their own learning, students are more likely to develop a sense of ownership and responsibility for their education, which can lead to better academic outcomes and a more fulfilling and well-rounded life.

Moreover, holistic education also promotes cultural and global understanding. It encourages students to learn about different cultures, religions, and traditions and to gain an understanding of the world beyond their immediate surroundings. This can help students to develop a sense of empathy and respect for different cultures.

6
Demeanor of Educator

The demeanor of an educator plays a crucial role in creating a positive and effective learning environment for students. A teacher's attitude and behavior can have a significant impact on the motivation, engagement, and overall success of their students. Teachers are responsible not only for imparting knowledge and skills to their students but also for creating an atmosphere in the classroom that fosters learning and encourages students to reach their full potential.

One of the most important aspects of an educator's demeanor is their ability to create a positive and welcoming classroom environment. This includes building positive relationships with students, being approachable and supportive, and creating a sense of community within the classroom. When students feel comfortable and valued in the classroom, they are more likely to be engaged and motivated to learn. Research has shown that students who have positive relationships with their teachers are more likely to have better academic outcomes and to be more engaged in the learning process. This can be achieved through simple acts of kindness and respect, such as greeting students by name, showing an interest in their lives, and being available to help and support them.

Another important aspect of an educator's demeanor is their ability to effectively manage the classroom. This includes setting clear expectations and consequences for behavior, being consistent and fair in their discipline, and creating a structured and organized learning environment. An effective classroom-management approach can help to reduce distractions and disruptions, which can lead to increased focus and engagement in students. A teacher's ability to maintain order and discipline in the classroom can help to create a safe and positive learning environment for students, which is essential for their academic and social development.

Additionally, an educator's demeanor should also reflect their passion for teaching and their subject matter. When educators are excited and enthusiastic about what they are teaching, it can be contagious and inspire students to be more engaged and motivated in their learning. This can be achieved by incorporating real-world examples and current events, creating hands-on activities, and encouraging critical thinking and class discussion. When students see that their teachers are passionate and excited about the subject matter, they are more likely to be engaged and to develop a love of learning.

Furthermore, an educator's demeanor should also reflect their ability to be an effective communicator. This includes being able to effectively explain concepts, provide feedback and answer questions, and encourage active participation from students. An educator that can communicate effectively can help students to better understand the material and to be more engaged in the learning process. This can be achieved by using clear and concise language, providing visual aids, and encouraging class participation through group work and class discussions.

It's also important for educators to be aware of their own biases and stereotypes and to make an effort to be inclusive and respectful of all students. This means creating a safe and inclusive environment for all students, regardless of their race, gender, religion, or sexual orientation. An inclusive classroom environment can help to promote positive relationships between students and to reduce the potential for discrimination and bullying. This can be achieved by providing a safe space for all students to share their perspectives, encouraging diversity and inclusion through classroom activities, and creating an environment where all students feel respected and valued.

Moreover, an educator's demeanor should also reflect their ability to adapt to the needs of their students. This means being able to differentiate instruction and to provide accommodations for students with special needs. Additionally, an educator should be able to recognize when a student is struggling and to provide support and guidance to help them succeed. This can be achieved by providing extra help, creating small group instruction, and providing accommodations such as extra time on exams or assistive technology.

I know it may sound odd to some – others will completely agree – but I've always found part of the correct demeanor for a teacher to be laughter and using fun in the classroom.

Laughter is a universal human experience that has the power to create connections, relieve stress, and promote happiness. In the educational setting, laughter can serve as a valuable tool for teachers to create a positive, welcoming environment for their students. Teachers who use laughter as a part of their demeanor can build stronger relationships with their students, help reduce anxiety and tension, and make learning more enjoyable and engaging.

One of the key benefits of incorporating laughter into the classroom is the ability to create a sense of community among students. When students are able to laugh and share experiences together, they become more comfortable with one another and are more likely to engage in meaningful discussions and group activities. This can be particularly helpful in diverse classrooms where students may come from different cultural or socioeconomic backgrounds.

Laughter can also be used as a way to reduce stress and anxiety in the classroom. Research has shown that laughter can help to reduce levels of cortisol, which is a hormone associated with stress. When students are less stressed, they are better able to focus on the material being taught and are more likely to retain the information.

In addition, a classroom that incorporates humor and playfulness can create a more relaxed atmosphere, which can help students feel more at ease and open to learning.

Another important benefit of using laughter in the classroom is the ability to make learning more enjoyable and engaging. When teachers use humor and playfulness to teach new concepts, students are more likely to remember the information and be interested in learning more. Additionally, students who enjoy learning are more likely to take ownership of their education and be motivated to succeed.

In order to incorporate laughter into their demeanor, teachers can use a variety of strategies, such as telling jokes, using humorous anecdotes, or incorporating fun activities into their lessons. Teachers can also encourage their students to share jokes or humorous stories, which can help to build a sense of community and create a fun, supportive atmosphere in the classroom. In addition to creating a positive classroom environment, laughter can also have a positive impact on teacher–student relationships. When teachers use humor and playfulness in their interactions with students, they can build stronger, more positive relationships with them. This can help to create a sense of trust and respect that can make it easier for students to approach their teachers with questions or concerns.

However, it's important to note that using laughter in the classroom should be done in a way that is appropriate and respectful. Teachers should be mindful of their audience and avoid humor that is divisive or offensive. Additionally, it's important to strike a balance between using humor to create a positive learning environment and maintaining a level of professionalism and respect for the subject matter being taught.

Incorporating laughter into their demeanor can be an important part of a teacher's approach to education. By creating a positive, welcoming classroom environment, reducing stress and anxiety, making learning more enjoyable and engaging, and building stronger relationships with their students, teachers who use laughter as a tool can have a positive impact on student success and well-being. However, it's important to use humor in a way that is appropriate and respectful and to maintain a balance between humor and professionalism in the classroom.

7

Assessment

In this book, we're talking about two different contexts for assessment: assessment in a classroom and assessment in a training situation. While there are clear overlaps, there are differences that will lead an autistic individual to gain success going into adulthood and career advancement. In this chapter, we're going to dive into a few different types of assessment used in education. I think they all have their place, but it's so important to note that every student is different! You may want to use and understand each and remember it's evolving for the success of each student. Please don't get caught up in a conclusion but constantly keep assessing.

Assessments in the classroom are an integral part of the learning process, as they provide a way to measure and evaluate the acquisition of knowledge and skills. The use of assessments in education can help identify areas of strength and weakness as well as providing feedback to both the learner and the instructor. However, not all assessments are created equal, and different types of assessments can have varying levels of value in terms of measuring and promoting the acquisition of skills.

Summative Assessment

Summative assessments provide important information about what a student has learned over a longer period of time and can help teachers and administrators make important decisions

DOI: 10.4324/9781003353959-9

about student progress, instructional effectiveness, and program improvement. In this section, we will examine different types of summative assessments, their purposes, and best practices for their use in education.

Types of Summative Assessments

There are many different types of summative assessments that educators can use to evaluate student learning. Some of the most common include:

- Standardized Tests: These are tests that are created by external agencies and are administered to all students in a particular grade level or subject area. Standardized tests are often used to evaluate school and district performance and to compare student achievement across different schools and regions. They are usually administered at regular intervals, such as annually or biennially, and can cover a wide range of subject areas, including language arts, math, science, and social studies.
- End-of-Unit or End-of-Course Tests: These are tests that are administered at the end of a specific unit or course of study. They are designed to evaluate how well students have learned the material covered in the unit or course and can be used to inform instruction, identify areas where students need additional support, and evaluate the effectiveness of the instructional materials and methods used.
- Performance Tasks: These are assessments that require students to demonstrate their learning through the completion of a complex task or project. Performance tasks can be used to assess a wide range of skills and knowledge, including problem-solving, critical thinking, research, writing, and presentation skills. They can be designed to align with specific standards or learning objectives and can be used to evaluate student progress towards specific learning goals.
- Portfolios: These are collections of student work that are assembled over time and are used to demonstrate student

progress and achievement. Portfolios can include a variety of different types of work, such as essays, projects, artwork, and other assignments. They can be used to evaluate student learning across a wide range of subject areas and can be especially useful for evaluating progress in areas where traditional assessments may not be sufficient.
- Capstone Projects: These are projects that are typically completed at the end of a student's academic career and are designed to demonstrate mastery of a specific set of skills or knowledge. Capstone projects can be used to evaluate student learning across a wide range of subject areas and can be especially useful for evaluating progress in areas where traditional assessments may not be sufficient.
- High-Stakes Assessments: These are assessments that have significant consequences for students, teachers, or schools. For example, high-stakes assessments may be used to determine whether students graduate from high school or whether schools receive funding or accreditation. High-stakes assessments can be controversial, as they can put significant pressure on students and teachers and may not always accurately reflect student learning.

Best Practices for Using Summative Assessments

While summative assessments can provide important information about student learning, it is important to use them effectively to ensure that the information they provide is accurate and useful. Here are some best practices for using summative assessments in education:

- Align Assessments with Learning Goals: It is important to ensure that summative assessments are aligned with specific learning goals or standards. This helps ensure that the assessment accurately reflects what students have learned and can provide useful information for teachers and administrators.
- Provide Clear and Consistent Expectations: Students should understand what is expected of them on the

assessment and how their work will be evaluated. Teachers should provide clear and consistent instructions and criteria for evaluation to ensure that the assessment is fair and accurate.
- ◆ Use Multiple Measures of Assessment: To ensure that the assessment accurately reflects what students have learned, it is important to use multiple measures of assessment.

In summative assessment, students are evaluated on their overall performance and are graded based on a set of predetermined criteria. This type of assessment is often used at the end of a course, semester, or school year to determine a student's level of achievement and proficiency in a subject area.

One advantage of summative assessment is that it provides a clear and objective evaluation of a student's performance, which can be used to make decisions about placement, promotion, or graduation. It also helps to ensure that students are meeting academic standards and provides a benchmark for comparing the performance of different students or schools.

However, there are also some potential disadvantages of summative assessment. For example, it can be stressful for students who feel like they are being judged solely on their performance on a single test or project. It can also lead to a focus on test-taking skills rather than on true mastery of the subject matter and may not accurately reflect a student's overall understanding of a topic.

To address some of these concerns, educators have developed a range of strategies for conducting effective summative assessments. One approach is to include a variety of assessment methods, such as written tests, oral presentations, and projects, which can provide a more comprehensive picture of a student's abilities and achievements. Another strategy is to use rubrics or grading criteria that are transparent and clearly communicated to students, which can help to reduce stress and improve the accuracy of evaluations.

In addition, educators may also provide opportunities for students to engage in self-assessment and reflection, which can help to enhance their understanding of their own learning process and provide valuable feedback to guide their future efforts. For example, students may be asked to evaluate their own performance on an assignment or test, identify areas where they need to improve, and develop a plan for further study and practice.

Overall, summative assessment plays a critical role in education by providing a mechanism for evaluating student performance and determining whether academic standards are being met. However, it is important for educators to use a range of assessment methods, communicate clear grading criteria, and provide opportunities for self-reflection and improvement in order to ensure that summative assessments are accurate, fair, and meaningful for students.

Formative Assessment

Formative assessment provides many advantages that contribute to its widespread use and popularity in education. However, there are also some disadvantages that need to be considered.

Enhancing Student Learning
One of the main advantages of formative assessment is that it can enhance student learning. By receiving feedback throughout the learning process, students are able to identify areas where they need to improve and adjust their learning strategies accordingly. This allows students to stay on track and achieve their learning goals more effectively.

Identifying Gaps in Knowledge
Formative assessment can also be used to identify gaps in student knowledge. This can help teachers to identify areas where they need to provide more support and guidance to help students achieve their learning goals. By addressing these gaps in knowledge, teachers can ensure that students are better equipped to succeed in their future studies.

Encouraging Student Engagement

Formative assessment can also encourage student engagement in the learning process. By providing regular feedback, it encourages students to take an active role in their own learning. This can help to increase motivation and promote a positive attitude towards learning.

Informing Instructional Decisions

Formative assessment can also be used to inform instructional decisions. It provides feedback to teachers about student progress and understanding, so teachers can make informed decisions about how to adjust their teaching strategies to better support student learning.

Improving Student–Teacher Communication

Formative assessment can also improve student–teacher communication. By providing regular feedback, teachers can build stronger relationships with their students and understand their learning needs more effectively. This can help to create a more supportive and positive learning environment.

Supporting Differentiated Instruction

Formative assessment can also support differentiated instruction. By providing feedback to students throughout the learning process, teachers can identify their individual learning needs and adjust their teaching strategies accordingly. This can help to ensure that all students are able to achieve their learning goals, regardless of their starting point.

Disadvantages of Formative Assessment

Despite its many advantages, formative assessment also has some disadvantages that need to be considered.

Time- and Resource-Intensive

One of the main disadvantages of formative assessment is that it can be time- and resource-intensive. Providing regular feedback to students requires significant time and effort on the part of teachers, which can be challenging in a busy classroom environment.

Inconsistent Implementation
Formative assessment can also be inconsistently implemented. Teachers may not always have a clear understanding of how to use formative assessment effectively, which can lead to inconsistent implementation across different classrooms and schools.

Overemphasis on Testing
Another potential disadvantage of formative assessment is that it can lead to an overemphasis on testing. If teachers focus too much on assessing student progress and understanding, it can detract from other important aspects of the learning process, such as creativity, critical thinking, and problem solving.

Limited Scope
Formative assessment also has a limited scope. It is primarily focused on assessing student progress and understanding within a specific subject or topic area. It may not be able to capture a student's overall learning progress and development over time.

Formative assessment is a powerful tool that can help to enhance student learning, improve instructional practices, and promote a positive and supportive learning environment. By providing regular feedback to students throughout the learning process, teachers can help them to identify areas where they need to improve, adjust their learning strategies accordingly, and stay on track to achieve their learning goals.

Feedback in Formative Assessment
Feedback is an essential component of formative assessment. It is the process of providing information to students about their performance and progress towards learning goals. Feedback can come in different forms, such as written comments, verbal feedback, and grades. Feedback that is timely, specific, and actionable can help students understand their strengths and weaknesses and what they need to do to improve.

There are several principles that teachers can follow when giving feedback:

- Timely: Feedback should be given as soon as possible after a task is completed. This allows students to reflect on their performance while the task is still fresh in their minds.
- Specific: Feedback should be specific and related to the learning goals. Vague feedback such as "good job" or "needs improvement" does not provide students with enough information to make meaningful changes to their learning.
- Actionable: Feedback should provide students with clear and specific steps they can take to improve. For example, instead of simply saying, "Your essay needs more detail," a teacher could provide specific examples from the essay of where more detail is needed.
- Respectful: Feedback should be given in a respectful and supportive manner that acknowledges students' efforts and encourages them to continue learning.

In addition to teacher feedback, peer feedback can also be an effective form of formative assessment. When students provide feedback to each other, they not only benefit from receiving feedback but also learn to become better evaluators of their own work.

Advantages and Disadvantages of Formative Assessment

Formative assessment has several advantages:

- It supports student learning by providing ongoing feedback and opportunities for self-reflection.
- It helps teachers understand student progress and adjust instruction to meet student needs.
- It can motivate students by giving them a sense of control over their learning and helping them see their progress over time.
- It encourages a growth mindset by emphasizing that learning is a process and mistakes are opportunities for growth.

However, there are also some potential disadvantages to formative assessment:

- It can be time-consuming for teachers to provide ongoing feedback and monitor student progress.
- Students may become overwhelmed by the amount of feedback they receive and struggle to prioritize their learning.
- It can be challenging to ensure that the feedback is specific and actionable and not simply a list of corrections.
- Students may become overly focused on grades or feedback and lose sight of the larger learning goals.

Formative assessment is a powerful tool for supporting student learning and improving instruction. By providing ongoing feedback and opportunities for reflection, teachers can help students take an active role in their learning and make meaningful progress towards their goals.

To be effective, formative assessment should be integrated into daily instruction and aligned with learning goals. Teachers should use a variety of assessment methods to gain a comprehensive understanding of student learning and provide timely, specific, and actionable feedback.

While formative assessment requires time and effort on the part of teachers and students, the benefits can be significant. By supporting a growth mindset and emphasizing the process of learning, formative assessment can help students become more engaged, motivated, and successful learners.

Performance Assessment

Performance assessments, such as projects, presentations, and essays, are also valuable in promoting skills acquisition. These assessments require the learner to demonstrate their understanding of the material in a real-world setting and provide an opportunity for the learner to apply their knowledge and skills to solve problems or complete tasks. Performance assessment is an approach to evaluating student learning that focuses on assessing students' ability to apply knowledge and skills in real-world situations. It is an alternative to traditional forms of assessment, such as multiple-choice tests, and emphasizes the development of higher-order thinking skills, such as critical thinking, problem-solving, and creativity. In this chapter, we will explore the concept of performance assessment in education, its benefits and challenges, and best practices for implementing it in the classroom.

Performance assessment is a form of assessment that evaluates students' ability to apply knowledge and skills in authentic settings. Unlike traditional forms of assessment, which rely on standardized tests and multiple-choice questions, performance assessment requires students to demonstrate what they know and can do in a real-world context.

Performance assessments can take many forms, such as portfolios, case studies, simulations, and project-based assessments. The focus is on evaluating students' ability to apply knowledge and skills in practical, real-world situations rather than simply recalling facts or memorizing information.

Benefits of Performance Assessment

Performance assessment has several benefits for both students and teachers. Some of the key advantages of performance assessment include:

- Authentic Assessment: Performance assessment provides a more authentic measure of student learning because it evaluates students' ability to apply knowledge and skills in real-world contexts.
- Higher-Order Thinking Skills: Performance assessment promotes the development of higher-order thinking skills, such as critical thinking, problem-solving, and creativity.
- Personalized Learning: Performance assessment allows for personalized learning because it provides students with opportunities to explore their interests and apply their knowledge in meaningful ways.

- Student Engagement: Performance assessment can increase student engagement and motivation because it allows students to take ownership of their learning and see the relevance of what they are learning.
- Teacher Feedback: Performance assessment provides teachers with rich information about students' learning and can help them identify areas where students need additional support or enrichment.

Challenges of Performance Assessment

While performance assessment has many benefits, it also poses several challenges for teachers and students. Some of the key challenges of performance assessment include:

- Time: Performance assessment can be time-consuming for both teachers and students because it requires a significant amount of planning, preparation, and evaluation.
- Resources: Performance assessment may require additional resources, such as materials, equipment, and technology, which may not be available in all schools.
- Grading: Performance assessment can be challenging to grade because it involves subjective judgments about students' work.
- Standardization: Performance assessment can be challenging to standardize because each student's work is unique, making it difficult to compare student performance across different contexts.

Best Practices for Implementing Performance Assessment

Despite the challenges of performance assessment, there are several best practices that teachers can follow to ensure its success in the classroom. Some of these best practices include:

- Aligning Assessments with Learning Objectives: Performance assessments should be aligned with learning objectives and should reflect the knowledge and skills that students are expected to learn.

- Using Rubrics: Rubrics can help ensure that performance assessments are graded consistently and fairly. They can also provide students with clear expectations for their work.
- Providing Feedback: Performance assessments should be accompanied by timely and meaningful feedback that helps students understand their strengths and weaknesses and how they can improve.
- Using Technology: Technology can be used to enhance performance assessments by providing students with access to online resources, digital tools, and multimedia materials.
- Emphasizing Student Ownership: Performance assessment should emphasize student ownership of learning by giving students choices about what they learn and how they demonstrate their learning.
- Encouraging Collaboration: Performance assessment can be enhanced through collaboration, allowing students to work in teams to solve real-world problems and learn from each other.

Designing Performance Assessments

Performance assessments are a useful tool for measuring student learning, but they can be challenging to design. To ensure that performance assessments are effective, educators need to design them carefully. Here are some key considerations for designing effective performance assessments.

Identify the Key Learning Objectives

The first step in designing an effective performance assessment is to identify the key learning objectives that you want to measure. Performance assessments should align closely with the learning objectives of the course or unit and should be designed to measure the knowledge and skills that students are expected to acquire. Before designing the assessment, it is essential to carefully review the course content and identify the key concepts, skills, and knowledge that students need to master.

Consider the Context

The context in which the assessment will take place is an important consideration in designing an effective performance assessment. The assessment should be designed to be appropriate for the context in which it will be administered. For example, if the assessment is designed to measure students' ability to communicate effectively, it should be designed to be appropriate for the specific audience and purpose for which the communication is intended. Similarly, if the assessment is designed to measure students' ability to work collaboratively, it should be designed to be appropriate for the specific context in which the collaboration will take place.

Select Appropriate Assessment Methods

Performance assessments can take many forms, and it is important to select the appropriate assessment methods for the specific learning objectives being assessed. Some possible assessment methods include:

- Authentic Assessments: Authentic assessments require students to demonstrate their knowledge and skills in a real-world context. Examples of authentic assessments include project-based assessments, case studies, and simulations.
- Observational Assessments: Observational assessments involve observing students as they perform a task or activity. Examples of observational assessments include performance tasks, role-playing, and structured interviews.
- Product-Based Assessments: Product-based assessments require students to create a tangible product that demonstrates their learning. Examples of product-based assessments include research papers, presentations, and portfolios.
- Self-Assessments: Self-assessments require students to reflect on their own learning and evaluate their own performance. Examples of self-assessments include journals, learning logs, and self-evaluations.

The selection of assessment methods should be based on the learning objectives being assessed as well as the context in which the assessment will take place.

Establish Clear Criteria for Success

In order to be effective, performance assessments need to have clear criteria for success. Students need to know exactly what they are being evaluated on and what constitutes success. Clear criteria help students focus their efforts and ensure that the assessment is fair and unbiased. When developing the criteria for success, it is important to be specific and detailed. Ideally, the criteria should be communicated to students before the assessment takes place.

Provide Sufficient Time and Resources

Performance assessments can be time-consuming and resource-intensive, and it is important to provide students with sufficient time and resources to complete the assessment. Students may need additional time to complete the assessment as well as access to resources such as technology, books, and other materials. In addition, it is important to provide students with clear instructions and guidance on how to complete the assessment.

Provide Timely and Constructive Feedback

Performance assessments are only effective if students receive timely and constructive feedback on their performance. Feedback should be provided as soon as possible after the assessment and should be specific, detailed, and focused on areas for improvement. Feedback should also be constructive, emphasizing areas where students have done well and areas where they need to improve. Providing feedback is an important part of the assessment process and can help students to develop their skills and knowledge.

Feedback and Follow-Up

The feedback and follow-up process is a crucial aspect of performance assessment. Once the results have been collected and analyzed, it's important to provide timely and constructive feedback to the students. This feedback can be given in a variety of ways, such as one-on-one meetings, group discussions, written comments, or digital feedback tools.

The feedback should not only highlight the strengths and weaknesses of the student's performance but also provide suggestions for improvement. The feedback should be specific, measurable, and actionable. It should be clear and concise so that the student understands the areas that need improvement and the steps required to achieve improvement.

Furthermore, follow-up is necessary to ensure that the student has implemented the feedback provided and made progress in the areas identified for improvement. This follow-up can take the form of regular check-ins or assessments to track the student's progress and provide additional feedback.

Validity and Reliability

Performance assessments must be both valid and reliable to be effective in assessing student learning. Validity refers to the extent to which the assessment measures what it is supposed to measure. If a performance assessment is designed to measure a student's ability to write an essay, for example, it should not also measure their typing speed or their proficiency in a foreign language.

Reliability refers to the consistency and stability of the assessment over time and across different evaluators. A performance assessment that produces inconsistent results when administered multiple times or by different evaluators may not be reliable.

To ensure validity and reliability, performance assessments should be designed with clear learning objectives and criteria for evaluation. Rubrics and scoring guides should be developed to ensure consistency in scoring and evaluation. The assessments should be pilot-tested to identify any potential issues and ensure that they are measuring what they are intended to measure.

Technology and Performance Assessment

Technology has revolutionized the way performance assessments can be conducted. There are now a variety of digital tools and platforms available that can be used to design, deliver, and evaluate performance assessments. These tools can range from simple online quizzes to sophisticated simulations and virtual reality environments.

Technology-enabled performance assessments can be more engaging and interactive than traditional paper-based assessments, and they can provide immediate feedback to the student. Digital tools can also automate some aspects of the assessment process, such as scoring and data analysis, making it easier and faster to administer and evaluate assessments.

However, technology-enabled performance assessments also have some drawbacks. They may require specialized equipment or software, which can be expensive and difficult to access. Moreover, there may be concerns about the security and integrity of the assessments, particularly if they are administered online.

Ethics and Performance Assessment

Finally, it is important to consider the ethical implications of performance assessment in education. Performance assessments can be high-stakes, particularly if they are used for grading or admission to higher education programs. As such, it is critical to ensure that the assessments are fair, unbiased, and equitable.

Performance assessments should be designed to measure the skills and knowledge that are relevant to the learning objectives and not based on extraneous factors such as race, gender, or socioeconomic status. The assessments should be administered in a standardized manner to ensure consistency across all students, and evaluators should be trained to avoid bias in their scoring and evaluation.

Moreover, performance assessments should be conducted with the informed consent of the students and their families, and their confidentiality should be protected. Any data collected should be used only for the purposes of the assessment and not shared with third parties without the student's consent.

Self-Assessments

Self-assessments, self-reflection, and self-evaluation are also essential part of the learning process as they provide learners with an opportunity to evaluate their own understanding and progress.

Self-assessment is a process in which students evaluate their own work, abilities, and progress. It is an essential part of education that allows students to reflect on their learning, set goals, and take ownership of their academic progress. In this section, we will explore the value of self-assessment in education and discuss how it can be used to promote learning and growth.

Encourages Self-Reflection
Self-assessment encourages students to reflect on their own learning and progress. It prompts them to think about what they have learned, how they have learned it, and what they still need to learn. This process helps students become more self-aware and more in tune with their own strengths and weaknesses.

Promotes Ownership of Learning
Self-assessment promotes ownership of learning. When students are involved in the assessment process, they are more invested in their own learning. They take responsibility for their progress and are more likely to set goals and work towards them. This sense of ownership and responsibility can lead to increased motivation and engagement.

Provides Valuable Feedback
Self-assessment provides valuable feedback to both students and teachers. When students evaluate their own work, they are able to identify areas where they need to improve and set goals for themselves. Teachers can use this information to tailor their instruction to meet the needs of individual students. Additionally, self-assessment allows teachers to gain insight into how students are thinking about the material and where they may be struggling.

Develops Critical-Thinking Skills
Self-assessment develops critical-thinking skills. When students evaluate their own work, they are forced to think critically about what they have learned and how they can improve. This process encourages students to question their own assumptions, evaluate evidence, and draw their own conclusions.

Promotes Metacognition
Self-assessment promotes metacognition, or thinking about thinking. When students evaluate their own work, they are engaging in a process of self-reflection that requires them to think about how they learn and how they can improve. This process helps students become more aware of their own thinking processes and more able to regulate their own learning.

Supports Lifelong Learning
Self-assessment supports lifelong learning. When students are able to evaluate their own work and progress, they develop a sense of agency and control over their own learning. This sense of control can lead to a lifelong love of learning and a commitment to personal growth and development.

Fosters Self-Esteem
Self-assessment fosters self-esteem. When students are involved in the assessment process, they are able to take pride in their accomplishments and set goals for themselves. This process can lead to increased confidence and self-esteem.

Self-assessment is an essential part of education that promotes learning and growth. It encourages self-reflection, promotes ownership of learning, provides valuable feedback, develops critical-thinking skills, promotes metacognition, supports lifelong learning, and fosters self-esteem. By incorporating self-assessment into their teaching practice, teachers can help students become more self-aware, more motivated, and more engaged in their own learning.

Skills-Based Assessment
There are many different types of skills-based assessment, each of which is designed to evaluate specific skills and knowledge. Here are a few examples of common skills-based assessment types:

- Performance-Based Assessment: Performance-based assessment measures an individual's ability to perform a specific task or activity. This can include anything from

a written test to a hands-on demonstration of a skill or process.
- Portfolio Assessment: Portfolio assessment involves compiling a collection of work samples that demonstrate an individual's skills and knowledge in a given field. This can include written reports, presentations, and other work products that showcase an individual's abilities.
- Self-assessment: Self-assessment involves evaluating one's own skills and knowledge in a specific area. This can be a valuable tool for individuals who are looking to identify areas where they may need additional training or support.
- Peer assessment: Peer assessment involves having individuals evaluate the skills and knowledge of their peers. This can be a valuable tool for promoting collaboration and teamwork as well as for providing constructive feedback and support.

Designing and Implementing a Successful Skills-Based Assessment Program

To design and implement a successful skills-based assessment program, there are several key factors to consider. Here are some tips for getting started:

- Identify the Skills and Knowledge You Want to Assess: Before designing an assessment program, it is important to identify the specific skills and knowledge you want to evaluate. This will help you select the appropriate assessment tools and methods.
- Select Appropriate Assessment Methods: Once you have identified the skills and knowledge you want to assess, you can select the appropriate assessment methods. This may involve using a combination of performance-based assessments, portfolio assessments, self-assessments, and peer assessments.
- Provide Clear Instructions and Expectations: To ensure that assessments are conducted consistently and fairly,

it is important to provide clear instructions and expectations for each assessment method. This may involve providing detailed rubrics or scoring guides as well as clear instructions for completing each assessment task.
- Train Assessors: It is important to provide training to those who will be conducting the assessments to ensure that they are knowledgeable about the assessment methods and procedures. This may involve providing training on how to use assessment tools, how to score assessments, and how to provide feedback to learners.
- Analyze and Use Assessment Results: Once assessments are completed, it is important to analyze the results and use them to inform instruction and support. This may involve identifying areas where learners may need additional training or support as well as areas where instruction and support have been successful.
- Continuously Evaluate and Refine the Assessment Program: To ensure that the assessment program remains effective and relevant, it is important to continuously evaluate and refine it over time. This may involve soliciting feedback from learners, instructors, and assessors as well as making adjustments to assessment tools and methods based on the results of evaluations.

Skills-based assessment offers a comprehensive and practical approach to evaluating an individual's abilities and potential in a given field. By measuring practical skills and knowledge, skills-based assessment can provide a more accurate and meaningful evaluation of an individual's abilities and potential, which can help promote a more hands-on and experiential learning approach.

To design and implement a successful skills-based assessment program, it is important to identify the specific skills and knowledge you want to assess, select appropriate assessment methods, provide clear instructions and expectations, train assessors, analyze and use assessment results, and continuously evaluate and refine the assessment program over time. By following these steps, you can create an effective and meaningful assessment program that promotes learning and growth.

It's also important to note that the use of technology in assessments can also enhance the value of assessments in skills acquisition. For example, online quizzes and tests can provide immediate feedback to the student and allow for self-paced learning. In addition, the use of simulations and virtual reality can provide a more authentic and interactive learning experience, allowing students to apply their knowledge and skills in a simulated real-world setting.

The value of assessments in skills acquisition depends on the type of assessment used. Summative assessments are useful for measuring retention of knowledge, but formative, performance, and self-assessments provide more insight.

8

Deception Without Deceit

I feel like this is a very valuable lesson for clinicians, educators, or parents to truly understand. I know I spoke about it earlier too, so hopefully you've been looking forward to this section. There is a way to give someone who is learning something the feeling of control, and thus ownership, over a project, lesson, or task while still having them do exactly what is expected of them.

So often in settings where there are multiple learners, it can be overwhelming for the teacher. Especially, if they're using a pedagogical approach rather than an andragogical approach.

Deception is often associated with dishonesty and trickery, but it can also be used in a positive way in the realm of skilled trades education. Deception without deceit can be an effective teaching tool, allowing educators to engage students in a more meaningful way and help them learn difficult concepts.

Skilled trades education is often focused on teaching practical skills and hands-on experience, but there are still opportunities to incorporate deception without deceit in the classroom. By using creative teaching techniques, educators can create a more engaging and interactive learning experience for students.

One common use of deception in education is through the use of simulations of real work experience. These simulations are more authentic to employment. These activities involve creating a hypothetical scenario or situation that requires students to use critical-thinking skills and apply knowledge in a practical way. By immersing students in a simulated environment, educators can create a more engaging and interactive learning experience.

In skilled trades education, simulations and role-playing exercises can be particularly effective for teaching safety protocols and procedures. For example, a construction instructor might create a simulation in which students must navigate a construction site while avoiding potential hazards such as exposed electrical wiring or heavy equipment. By being immersed in this simulated environment, students can develop a better understanding of how to identify and avoid potential safety hazards in real-world situations.

Another way that simulations can be used in skilled trades education is by creating scenarios that require students to apply their knowledge of materials and techniques. For example, a welding instructor might create a simulation in which students must repair a piece of metal using a specific welding technique. Faced with a practical problem to solve, students can apply their knowledge in a more meaningful way and develop a deeper understanding of the welding process.

Another way that deception can be used in skilled trades education is through the use of games and puzzles. These activities often involve a level of mystery or intrigue that captures students' attention and encourages them to think creatively.

For example, a plumbing instructor might use a puzzle to teach students about the different types of pipes and fittings used in plumbing systems. The puzzle might involve a diagram of a plumbing system that has missing pieces, and students must identify the missing pieces and select the correct pipe or fitting to complete the system. This type of activity encourages students to think creatively and apply their knowledge in a practical way.

Another way that deception can be used in skilled trades education is through the use of storytelling. By weaving a narrative around a particular concept or idea, educators can create a more memorable and engaging learning experience.

For example, a carpentry instructor might use storytelling to teach students about the history of carpentry and the evolution of carpentry tools and techniques. The instructor might tell a story about a famous carpenter from history and use that story to illustrate the different tools and techniques that were used during that time period. This type of activity can help students develop a deeper appreciation for and understanding of the craft of carpentry and how it has evolved over time.

Finally, deception can be used in skilled trades education through the use of real-world examples and case studies. By presenting students with real-world scenarios and case studies, educators can help students understand how the concepts and techniques they are learning in the classroom can be applied in practical situations.

For example, an HVAC instructor might present a case study about a commercial building that is experiencing HVAC system failure. The case study might include information about the building's layout, the types of HVAC systems installed, and the symptoms of the system failure. Students would then be asked to analyze the case study and come up with a solution to the HVAC system failure. By working through this type of real-world scenario, students can develop a better understanding of how to apply their HVAC knowledge in a practical setting.

There are several benefits to using deception without deceit in skilled trades education. One of the primary benefits is that it can create a more engaging and interactive learning experience. By using simulations, games, illusions, storytelling, and case studies, educators can capture students' attention and help them develop a deeper understanding of the concepts and techniques they are learning.

Another benefit of using deception without deceit in skilled trades education is that it can help students develop critical-thinking skills. By presenting students with practical problems to solve, educators can encourage them to think creatively and apply their knowledge in a practical way. This type of activity can help students develop problem-solving skills that are essential in the skilled trades industry.

Using deception without deceit in skilled trades education can also help students develop a better appreciation for the craft they are learning. By using storytelling and historical examples, educators can help students understand the evolution of their craft and the important role it plays in society. This type of activity can help students develop a sense of pride in and ownership of their work, which can be a powerful motivator.

Deception without deceit can be a valuable tool in skilled trades education. By using simulations, games, illusions, storytelling, and case studies, educators can create a more engaging and interactive learning experience for students. This type of activity can help students develop critical-thinking skills, problem-solving skills, and a deeper appreciation for the craft they are learning. As skilled trades education continues to evolve, educators should consider using deception without deceit as a way to enhance the learning experience and help students develop the skills they need to succeed in the industry.

2
Training

9
Simulation Site

One of the steps I've found in setting up a successful transition into employment is setting up the learning environment to stimulate the work environment. Here's what I mean. At TACT, we teach trades and technical skills. Our workspaces are very industrial, loud, and dusty (but organized!); often smell like wood and motor oil; and are hot from making things with metal.

In today's job market, it's more important than ever for students to gain real-world experience in their chosen field before they graduate. One way to provide this experience is by setting up an educational site that simulates a job site. This type of educational site can give students a taste of what it's like to work in a particular industry and help them develop the skills they need to be successful in that field. In this guide, we'll walk through the steps of setting up an educational site to simulate a job site, including the planning, implementation, and ongoing maintenance phases.

Planning

The first step in setting up an educational site to simulate a job site is to plan the overall project. This includes identifying the goals of the project, determining the target audience, and identifying the resources that will be needed to make the project a success. Talk to your business partners and ask, "What are the skills young and new workers need to be successful?" They'll tell you because it's in their interest. So often, education and training are merely academic and do not translate to real work skills. Begin with the end in mind here. And if you set up the space to look, feel, sound, and smell like the environment they'll work in, it helps the transition become that much easier.

Goals

The goals of an educational site that simulates a job site will vary depending on the industry and the specific needs of the students. Some possible goals might include providing students with hands-on experience in a particular field, helping students develop specific skills, or giving students a taste of what it's like to work in a particular industry. But remember, it's on a one-by-one basis. Every student is different; please don't treat everyone the same. Remember what we said about deception without deceit! You can have multiple students engaged in different projects, all learning the same technical, social, and emotional skills.

Target Audience

The target audience for an educational site that simulates a job site will also vary depending on the industry and the specific needs of the students. This could include high school students, college students, or adult learners. What we mean by this is the trade; the trade and employer are your target audience. You don't teach carpentry the same way you would music, but work skills and work ethic can overlap.

Resources

The resources that will be needed to set up an educational site to simulate a job site will depend on the goals of the project and the target audience. Some possible resources might include funding for the project, a web development team, an employment team, and the educational team. They all need to work together and constantly communicate. The skills learned in the classroom setting should mirror the work site down to the tools, layout, task analysis, and communication style.

Implementation

Once the planning phase is complete, the next step is to implement the project. This includes building the site, creating the content, and launching the site to the target audience. This is your individualized education program (IEP) or employment plan, whatever your area calls it. It's your action to make it happen! Communication within your team to get this far is going to be paramount to making this successful.

Building the Site

The first step in building the site is to choose an employment and educational team. This team should have experience building educational sites and should be able to create a site that meets the goals of the project. The site should be easy to navigate and should be designed to be accessible to the target audience. They need to know the trades and employment system and be like-minded in their strengths-based approach to education. If not – and if they're a deficit-type person – it's really hard.

Creating the Content

The next step is to create the content (a.k.a., curriculum) for the training setting. This includes creating the text, images, and videos that will be used on the site – everything they need to be successful. The content should be engaging and should be designed to meet the goals of the project and keep it focused on the individual. It can't have the traditional pedagogical focus;

it's not about you – it's about them! The content should also be accessible and differentiated in approach. Many Medicaid funding streams make that mandatory, so please keep it in that vein.

Launching Your Training Program

Once the site is built and the content is created, the next step is to launch the site to the community. This will be the hardest part. It takes a lot of time, money, and resources to get this far, but if you've dug deep to get here, you're on the right track.

Ongoing Maintenance

An educational site that simulates a job site is not a one-time project; it's an ongoing one. It's important to continuously update the site with new content, fix any technical issues, and make changes based on feedback from the target audience. This will ensure that the site continues to meet the goals of the project and provide a valuable experience to students.

10

Failure to Succeed

For some reason, this is a controversial thought. I've never understood that and disagree with those who don't let students fail. Or employees, for that matter. It's such an absolutely critical part of growth – not only that, but remembering the failure, the feeling of it and, ultimately, the triumph over it. Many successful people attribute their achievements to the lessons they learned from their failures. Failure can be a valuable learning experience and can ultimately lead to success.

One way that failure can lead to success is by teaching valuable lessons about perseverance and determination. When faced with failure, individuals must learn to pick themselves up and try again. This resilience and determination can be invaluable in achieving success in the future. For example, Thomas Edison is known for having failed over a thousand times before finally inventing the light bulb. He famously said, "I have not failed. I've just found 10,000 ways that won't work." This perseverance and determination is one of the reasons he was able to achieve such great success.

Failure can also teach important lessons about problem-solving and creativity. When faced with failure, individuals must learn to think outside the box and come up with new and innovative solutions. This ability to think creatively and solve problems is essential to achieving success in any field. For example, when Steve Jobs was fired from Apple, the company he cofounded, he went on to start a new company, Pixar, which revolutionized the animation industry and was eventually sold for $7.4 billion. His experience of failure and the need to think creatively led to even greater success.

Another way that failure can lead to success is by helping individuals to develop a growth mindset. A growth mindset is a belief that one's abilities can be developed and improved through effort and learning. By embracing failure and viewing it as an opportunity to learn and grow, individuals can develop a growth mindset that will serve them well in their future pursuits. Failure can help individuals to realize that their abilities are not fixed and that they have the power to improve and succeed.

Failure can also help individuals to learn the importance of humility and self-reflection. Successful individuals often credit their failures with helping them to become more humble and self-aware. This humility and self-awareness can help individuals to be more in tune with their own strengths and weaknesses, allowing them to make better decisions in the future. For example, after a failed product launch, Mark Zuckerberg, the CEO of Facebook, took the time to reflect on his mistakes and make changes to the company's strategy. This humility and self-reflection helped to turn Facebook into the successful company it is today.

Additionally, failure can help individuals to learn the importance of taking calculated risks. Oftentimes, success is the result of taking risks and stepping out of one's comfort zone. Failure can help individuals to learn when it is appropriate to take risks and when it is not. Failure can also teach individuals to be more strategic in the risks they take by learning to identify potential obstacles and developing plans to mitigate them.

Finally, failure can also be a great teacher of patience. When faced with failure, individuals must learn to be patient and persistent in their pursuit of success. This patience and persistence can be invaluable in achieving long-term success. Failure can teach individuals to understand that success is not always immediate and that it takes time and patience to achieve.

In addition to these general ways, failure can teach other specific lessons as well. It can teach individuals to be more resilient, to be more adaptable, to be more strategic, and to be more openminded. Failure can also help individuals to develop a sense of self-awareness and to understand the importance of self-care, and it can help individuals to learn the importance of being able to accept constructive criticism and to use it to improve.

It's important to note that failure is not always a negative experience. It can also be a positive one if it's viewed in the right way.

11
Holistic Approach

In traditional autism education, everything segmented – and, truthfully, in neurotypical education too, just not to the same degree. For example, math is taught separately from science, physical education separately from English, etc. But why? In autism education, they have traditionally broken things down as far as teaching eye contact or toe-walking separately from communication or socialization. Why? That's not the way people learn, and it shouldn't be the way things are taught. Holistic education is an approach to learning that focuses on the development of the whole person rather than just their academic or intellectual abilities. This approach emphasizes the importance of creating well-rounded individuals who are able to think critically, communicate effectively, and be responsible global citizens.

A holistic education includes a wide range of subjects and activities, including traditional academic subjects such as math, science, and literature as well as physical education, the arts, and practical life skills. This approach to education recognizes that there are many different ways that individuals learn and that all of these ways are important.

One key aspect of holistic education is the emphasis on critical thinking and problem-solving skills. This approach encourages students to think critically about the information they are presented with and to question assumptions. It also encourages students to approach problems in a creative and analytical way and to look for multiple solutions. This is important as it helps students to develop the ability to think independently and to question the information they are given, which is essential for lifelong learning.

Another important aspect of holistic education is the emphasis on emotional and social development. This approach recognizes that individuals must be able to manage their emotions and interact effectively with others in order to be successful in life. Holistic education includes activities and subjects that help students to develop their emotional intelligence and social skills, such as conflict resolution, emotional regulation, and effective communication. It also includes the development of empathy, compassion, and understanding toward others, which are essential in building a more inclusive and harmonious society.

Holistic education also emphasizes the importance of physical health and wellness. This approach includes physical education and activities that promote physical fitness and health, such as yoga, sports, and outdoor education. Additionally, holistic education also teaches about healthy eating, hygiene and personal care, and the impact of physical well-being on mental and emotional well-being. Physical health is an important foundation for overall well-being, and holistic education ensures that students develop habits that promote physical health and well-being, which will serve them well throughout their lives.

Holistic education also places a strong emphasis on the importance of the arts and the humanities. This approach recognizes the value of creativity, imagination, and self-expression and encourages students to explore their artistic and creative abilities. It also recognizes the importance of the humanities, such as history, philosophy, and ethics, in helping individuals to understand themselves and the world around them. The arts and humanities can help students to develop their creativity, imagination, and self-expression, which are essential for personal growth and development. They also help students to develop an appreciation for different cultures, which is essential for understanding and accepting diversity in the world.

Finally, holistic education also emphasizes the importance of civic engagement and social responsibility. This approach encourages students to think about how their actions can impact the world around them and to take an active role in addressing social and environmental issues. It also encourages students to think about the importance of global citizenship and to be aware of the issues and challenges facing the world today. This approach helps students to develop a sense of responsibility towards their community, society, and the planet and to understand the impact of their actions on the world.

A story we get a lot at TACT is something similar to the story of John. As a child, John was always "different" from his peers. He struggled to make friends and often felt overwhelmed by the sensory stimuli around him. It wasn't until he was six years old that he was diagnosed with autism. (Which isn't that unusual since there is a two-year waiting list in most diagnostic facilities.)

John's parents were determined to provide him with the best possible education, but they found that traditional schools were not equipped to meet his needs. John was often misunderstood by his teachers and classmates, and he struggled to keep up with the demands of the curriculum.

It wasn't until John's parents discovered a school that specialized in holistic education that they found a solution. The school focused on providing a well-rounded education that emphasized not only academic achievement but also personal growth and development. The staff understood that every child was unique and had individual needs, and they were committed to creating a supportive and inclusive environment.

When John first started at the school, he was hesitant and anxious. He was used to feeling like an outsider, and he didn't know how to navigate the new environment. However, the staff quickly recognized his strengths and worked with him to create a personalized plan that would help him thrive.

One of the first things that John's teachers did was to incorporate sensory integration therapy into his daily routine. They recognized that John was easily overwhelmed by certain sensory stimuli, and they wanted to help him develop coping mechanisms. Through a series of exercises and activities, John learned how to regulate his sensory input and cope with his environment more effectively.

The school also emphasized social-emotional learning, which was a gamechanger for John. In traditional schools, he had always struggled to make friends and connect with his classmates. However, at this new school, he was surrounded by staff and students who valued kindness, empathy, and understanding. John was able to form meaningful connections with his peers, and he learned how to communicate his thoughts and feelings in a way that was understood by others.

Another area of focus at the school was project-based learning. John had always been interested in science, and he was fascinated by the natural world. The staff recognized his passion and worked with him to create a project that allowed him to explore his interests. He spent weeks researching different ecosystems and animal habitats, and he even created his own miniature ecosystem in the classroom. Through this project, John learned about science, but he also developed critical-thinking skills and problem-solving abilities.

Finally, the school incorporated mindfulness and meditation into the curriculum. John had always struggled with anxiety, and he often found it difficult to focus on his work. However, learning who he was and that it was okay to be himself, he learned how to calm his mind and stay present in the moment. He was able to use these techniques in other areas of his life, and he found that he was better able to manage his anxiety and stress levels.

Over time, John's parents noticed a significant change in him. He was more confident, more engaged, and more enthusiastic about learning. He had developed a love of science, and he was excited about exploring new ideas and concepts. He had also made friends, and he felt like he was a part of a community.

When John graduated from the school, he was better prepared for the challenges of the future. He had developed a strong foundation in academics, but he had also learned important life skills like communication and problem-solving. He was confident in his abilities, and he knew that he could achieve whatever he set his mind to.

In a holistic education approach, teachers act as facilitators who guide students in their learning journey rather than just providing information. They encourage students to take an active role in their own learning and to explore and discover new things. Teachers also use a variety of teaching methods to cater to different learning styles and to ensure that all students have an opportunity to learn in a way that suits them best.

Holistic education also values the importance of experiential learning, where students are encouraged to learn through practical and hands-on experiences.

12

Slow to Go Fast

Going slow to move quickly is a concept that applies not just to education but to many aspects of life. In the context of neurodivergent education, it means taking the time to understand and accommodate the unique needs and strengths of each individual student rather than trying to fit them into a one-size-fits-all mold. With our population, it's all about relationships, and, going slow, you will build those!

In Education

One of the key reasons going slow is important in neurodivergent education is that it allows for a more personalized approach to learning. Every student is different and has their own unique set of strengths and weaknesses. By taking the time to understand these differences and tailor instruction to meet the needs of each individual student, educators can help ensure that each student is able to learn in a way that is most effective for them.

Another important aspect of going slow in neurodivergent education is the emphasis on building strong relationships between educators and students. When educators take the time to get to know their students, they are better able to understand their unique needs and strengths. This understanding can then be used to create a more positive and supportive learning environment for all students.

In addition to building stronger relationships and providing more personalized instruction, going slow in neurodivergent education also allows for greater flexibility in the classroom. When educators take the time to understand the unique needs of each student, they are better able to adapt their teaching methods and materials to meet those needs. This can include using different teaching styles, providing extra support, or modifying assignments and assessments.

Moreover, going slow in neurodivergent education can also help to increase student engagement and motivation. When students feel that their needs are being met and that they are being understood, they are more likely to be engaged in the learning process. This can lead to better academic performance and a more positive overall experience for students.

Going slow in neurodivergent education also allows educators to identify and support students who may be struggling. By providing extra support and accommodations, educators can help ensure that all students are able to succeed academically. This can include providing extra time for assignments, allowing for the use of assistive technology, or providing one-on-one instruction.

Going slow in neurodivergent education can also help to promote inclusivity and equity in the classroom. When educators take the time to understand and accommodate the unique needs of all students, they are better able to create a learning environment that is inclusive and welcoming to all. This can help to promote a sense of belonging and acceptance among all students regardless of their neurodivergent status.

Going slow to move quickly is a vital concept in neurodivergent education. By taking the time to understand and accommodate the unique needs and strengths of each individual student, educators can help ensure that all students are able to learn in a way that is most effective for them. This can lead to better academic performance, greater student engagement and motivation, and a more inclusive and equitable learning environment for all.

In the Workplace

To look at it from an employer's perspective, you'll also want to pick your employee partners closely. In today's fast-paced world, businesses are under pressure to deliver results quickly. When it comes to onboarding new employees, this often means cutting corners and rushing through the training process. However, research shows that taking the time to properly train and set up employees leads to better results in the long run. In this section, we will explore why good training and setup for an employee, which takes longer and is slow, leads to better results in the long run.

Good training is the foundation for a successful employee. It provides the knowledge, skills, and confidence necessary to perform job duties effectively. Without proper training, employees are likely to struggle and may not meet performance expectations. This can lead to frustration for both the employee and the employer. Good training also sets expectations for employees. They know what is expected of them, how they should perform their job duties, and what standards they need to meet. This clarity leads to a sense of purpose and direction, which can motivate employees to perform at their best. Additionally, good training can improve employee retention. When employees feel supported and equipped to perform their jobs, they are more likely to stay with the company long-term. This can save the business money on recruitment and training costs in the long run.

Taking longer to train and set up employees may seem counterintuitive. After all, businesses are under pressure to deliver results quickly. However, taking the time to properly train and set up employees can actually save time and money in the long run.

When employees are rushed through training, they may not fully understand their job duties or how to perform them effectively. This can lead to mistakes, errors, and inefficiencies. These mistakes can be costly in terms of time, money, and customer satisfaction. By taking the time to properly train employees, businesses can prevent these mistakes from occurring in the first place. Additionally, taking longer to train employees can actually save time in the long run. When employees are properly trained, they are more efficient and productive. They are able to perform their job duties effectively, which means they can complete tasks more quickly. This can save time and increase output in the long run.

Starting slow may seem counterintuitive in today's fast-paced world. However, when it comes to onboarding new employees, being slow can actually lead to better results in the long run. Starting slow means taking the time to properly set up new employees. This includes providing them with the tools, resources, and support they need to perform their job duties effectively. By being slow, businesses can ensure that employees are properly equipped to perform their jobs.

Starting slow also means taking the time to get to know employees. This includes understanding their strengths, weaknesses, and learning styles. By taking the time to get to know employees, businesses can tailor their training to meet their individual needs. This can lead to more effective training and better long-term results.

Why Investing in Employees Is Important

Investing in employees is important because it shows them that they are valued. When businesses invest in their employees, they are more likely to feel engaged, motivated, and committed to their jobs. This can lead to better performance, higher job satisfaction, and increased employee retention.

Investing in employees can also lead to improved customer satisfaction. When employees are properly trained and equipped to perform their job duties, they are more likely to provide excellent customer service. This can lead to repeat business and positive word-of-mouth advertising. Additionally, investing in employees can lead to innovation and growth. When employees are given the tools, resources, and support they need to perform their jobs effectively, they are more likely to come up with new ideas and solutions. This can lead to improved processes, increased efficiency, and better results in the long run.

Furthermore, investing in employees can lead to a positive workplace culture. When employees feel supported and valued, they are more likely to collaborate, communicate effectively, and work towards shared goals. This can lead to a more cohesive and productive team.

Investing in employees also helps businesses to stay competitive in the market. When businesses have well-trained and capable employees, they are better equipped to meet the demands of the market. This can lead to increased sales, improved customer satisfaction, and a stronger reputation.

Moreover, investing in employees can lead to a reduction in costs associated with employee turnover. When employees are properly trained and supported, they are more likely to stay with the company long-term. This can save the business money on recruitment and training costs as well as prevent a loss of productivity that often comes with employee turnover.

In the United States, there are many examples of businesses that have seen the benefits of good training and setup for employees. One such example is Southwest Airlines. Southwest Airlines is known for its excellent customer service and has consistently been ranked as one of the best airlines in the United States. This is due in large part to the company's investment in its employees. Southwest Airlines provides extensive training for its employees, including customer service training, safety training, and technical training. The company also encourages its employees to be themselves and to have fun on the job. This leads to a positive workplace culture and motivated employees.

Another example of good training and setup for employees is Google. Google is known for its innovative and collaborative workplace culture. The company invests heavily in its employees, providing them with training, resources, and support to perform their jobs effectively. Google also encourages its employees to be creative and to take risks. This leads to new ideas and innovations that have helped the company stay competitive in the market. Additionally, Google provides a range of perks and benefits to its employees, including free meals, onsite fitness classes, and opportunities for professional development.

Good training and setup for employees is essential for long-term success in business. Taking the time to properly train and set up employees can lead to improved performance, increased efficiency, and better customer satisfaction. Investing in employees also leads to a positive workplace culture, increased innovation, and a competitive edge in the market. Therefore, businesses should prioritize good training and setup for their employees, even if it means taking longer and being slow at the outset. In the long run, this investment will pay off with better results and a stronger, more motivated workforce.

13

Setup of Training

Skills-based training is a vital component of preparing teens and young adults for their future careers. By equipping them with the skills they need to succeed in today's job market, we can help ensure that they have the best possible chance of finding fulfilling and well-paying work.

The traditional education system often focuses on theoretical concepts and does not always prepare students for the real-world job market. Skills-based training programs have been proven to be more effective in providing students with the skills and knowledge they need to succeed in their chosen careers. In this chapter, we will discuss the key elements of setting up a successful skills-based training program for teens and young adults.

Identifying the Skills in Demand

The first step in setting up a skills-based training program is to identify the skills that are in demand in today's job market. This can be done by researching job listings, talking to industry experts, and consulting with local businesses. It is important to keep in mind that the job market is constantly changing, and what may be in demand today may not be in demand in the future. Therefore, it is essential to regularly review and update the skills being taught to ensure that they align with current job market trends. Some of the most in-demand skills for teens and young adults include cyber security, electrical pre-manufacturing, and maintenance and repair.

Developing Curriculum

Once you have identified the skills that are in demand, the next step is to develop a curriculum that will teach those skills to your students. It is important to keep in mind that the curriculum should be hands-on and focus on practical skills that students can use in the real world. Additionally, it should be flexible and adaptable to the needs of your students. This means that it should be designed to accommodate different learning styles and abilities. The curriculum should also be designed to provide students with the opportunity to learn at their own pace as well as the opportunity to apply what they have learned in real-world scenarios.

Finding Instructors

The next step is to find instructors who have the knowledge and experience to teach the skills you have identified. It is important to find instructors who are passionate about the subject matter and who have experience working in the industry. This ensures that they can provide students with up-to-date information and insights into the latest industry trends. Additionally, they should be able to connect the material with real-world examples and be able to provide individual attention. This will help students understand the material better and allow them to apply it to their own lives.

Here are some tips to help you find the right instructor for you.

Ask for Recommendations

The best way to find a good instructor is to ask for recommendations from friends, family, and colleagues who have experience with the subject matter. Ask them about their experiences with the recommended instructors, what they liked and didn't like about them, and what they learned from the classes. This will give you an idea of the instructors' teaching style, the difficulty level of the classes, and the overall quality of the instruction.

Research the Instructors
Once you have some recommendations, do your own research on the instructors. Look up their credentials and experience in the field, read reviews or testimonials from other students, and find out if they have published any articles or books on the subject. This will help you get a better sense of their teaching style and whether it aligns with your learning preferences.

Attend a Trial Class
Before committing to a full course, attend a trial class with the instructor. This will give you the opportunity to see their teaching style in action and gauge whether it works for you. Pay attention to the instructor's pace, tone of voice, and level of engagement with the students. Do they create a positive and inclusive learning environment? Do they challenge students to think critically and encourage participation?

Consider the Subject/Skill Format
Another important factor to consider is the course format. Some instructors are better suited to one-on-one instruction, while others excel in a classroom setting. Similarly, some instructors may be better suited to online instruction, while others may prefer in-person teaching. Make sure the instructor's teaching style aligns with the course format that you prefer.

Check for Professionalism
Finally, it's important to choose an instructor who is professional, punctual, and communicative. This means that they show up on time for class, are responsive to student questions and concerns, and maintain a professional demeanor at all times. A good instructor will also be organized and prepared with clear course objectives and a well-planned curriculum that's in line with the goals of the behavior plan, IEP, or student objectives.

Finding a good instructor takes time and effort, but it's well worth it in the end. By following these tips, you'll be well on your way to finding an instructor who will inspire, challenge, and motivate you to succeed. Remember, the right instructor can make all the difference in your learning experience.

Building a Supportive Environment

Building a supportive classroom environment is a crucial aspect of creating a positive and effective learning experience for students. A supportive classroom environment is one that promotes positive interactions among students and between students and their teachers. Such an environment encourages open communication, promotes mutual respect, and fosters a sense of belonging among all students. In this section, we will explore different strategies that educators can use to create a supportive classroom environment that is conducive to learning.

Establish Clear Expectations

Setting clear expectations is the first step in building a supportive classroom environment. Teachers should communicate to their students what they expect in terms of behavior, performance, and attitude. This can be done through class rules, a syllabus, and grading criteria. When students know what is expected of them, they are more likely to follow those expectations and contribute positively to the classroom environment.

Encourage Positive Interactions

Positive interactions between students and their teachers, as well as among students, are essential to building a supportive classroom environment. Teachers should encourage positive interactions by modeling respectful communication, active listening, and empathy. They should also provide opportunities for students to work collaboratively and to engage in discussions where they can share their thoughts and ideas.

Foster a Sense of Belonging

A supportive classroom environment is one where students feel a sense of belonging. Teachers can create a sense of belonging by recognizing and valuing the diversity of their students, by providing opportunities for students to share their personal experiences and perspectives, and by creating a safe and inclusive space where students feel comfortable expressing themselves.

Promote Active Learning

Active learning is an approach that encourages students to take an active role in their own learning. This can be achieved through a variety of strategies, including group work, discussions, problem-solving activities, and project-based learning. By promoting active learning, teachers can create an environment that encourages students to think critically, to collaborate, and to learn from one another.

Provide Timely and Meaningful Feedback

Feedback is a critical component of the learning process. It provides students with information about their progress and helps them identify areas where they need to improve. Teachers should provide timely and meaningful feedback that is specific, actionable, and supportive. This can help students stay motivated, improve their performance, and feel more confident in their abilities.

Create a Safe and Positive Learning Environment

A safe and positive learning environment is essential to building a supportive classroom environment. Teachers can create a safe and positive learning environment by establishing clear rules and consequences for behavior, by providing a physical space that is clean and well maintained, and by encouraging students to take responsibility for their own learning and behavior.

Use Technology to Enhance Learning

Technology can be a powerful tool for enhancing learning and creating a supportive classroom environment. Teachers can use technology to provide students with access to a wide range of resources, to facilitate communication and collaboration, and to create engaging and interactive learning experiences.

Build Strong Relationships With Students
Building strong relationships with students is key to creating a supportive classroom environment. Teachers should take the time to get to know their students on a personal level, to understand their strengths and weaknesses, and to provide support and encouragement when needed. By building strong relationships with their students, teachers can create an environment where students feel valued, respected, and supported.

Encourage Student Voice and Choice
Encouraging student voice and choice is an important strategy for building a supportive classroom environment. Teachers should provide opportunities for students to make choices about their learning, to express their opinions and ideas, and to take ownership of their own learning. This can help students feel more engaged and invested in their learning and can lead to improved performance and outcomes.

Continuously Reflect and Adapt
Creating a supportive classroom environment is an ongoing process that requires continuous reflection and adaptation. Teachers should regularly reflect on their teaching practices and their interactions with students and make adjustments as needed to ensure that they are creating an environment that is conducive to learning and growth.

Address Bullying and Harassment
Bullying and harassment can have a devastating impact on students and can disrupt the classroom environment. Teachers should take a proactive approach to addressing bullying and harassment by establishing clear policies and procedures for reporting and addressing such behaviors. They should also provide resources and support for students who have been impacted by bullying and harassment.

Celebrate Diversity and Inclusion
Celebrating diversity and inclusion is an important aspect of building a supportive classroom environment. Teachers should

recognize and value the diversity of their students and should create opportunities for students to learn about and appreciate different cultures and perspectives. This can help students develop empathy and understanding and can create a more inclusive and supportive classroom environment.

Foster a Growth Mindset

A growth mindset is an attitude that emphasizes the importance of effort, persistence, and learning from mistakes. Teachers can foster a growth mindset by encouraging students to take risks, to embrace challenges, and to view mistakes as opportunities for learning and growth. By fostering a growth mindset, teachers can create an environment that is supportive of student learning and that promotes a positive attitude towards learning and growth.

Provide Opportunities for Student Leadership

Providing opportunities for student leadership is an important strategy for building a supportive classroom environment. Teachers should provide opportunities for students to take on leadership roles, to make decisions about their learning, and to collaborate with their peers. This can help students develop leadership skills, build confidence, and feel more invested in their learning.

Engage Parents and Families

Engaging parents and families in the learning process is an important aspect of building a supportive classroom environment. Teachers should communicate regularly with parents and families, providing updates on student progress and opportunities for involvement in the classroom. This can help parents and families feel more connected to their child's learning and can create a more supportive and collaborative learning environment.

Building a supportive classroom environment is a complex process that requires a range of strategies and approaches. By establishing clear expectations, promoting positive interactions, fostering a sense of belonging, promoting active learning, providing timely and meaningful feedback, creating a safe and positive learning environment, using technology to enhance learning, building strong relationships with students, encouraging student voice and choice, continuously reflecting and adapting, addressing bullying and harassment, celebrating diversity and inclusion, fostering a growth mindset, providing opportunities for student leadership, and engaging parents and families, teachers can create a learning environment that is supportive, inclusive, and conducive to growth and development.

Measuring Success

While skills-based learning has become an increasingly popular approach to education in recent years, particularly in industries and professions where practical skills and knowledge are highly valued, it's not a traditional method of teaching. Thus, even the most seasoned teachers may feel out of place. Unlike traditional academic programs, which focus primarily on theoretical knowledge and concepts, skills-based learning programs are designed to provide students with the practical skills and experience they need to succeed in their chosen industry or profession.

However, measuring success in skills-based learning can be a complex and challenging task. Success can be defined in many different ways and can vary depending on the individual student's goals and needs. In this section, we will explore some of the key factors that contribute to success in skills-based learning and offer strategies for measuring success in this context.

Factors to Consider When Measuring Success in Skills-Based Learning
Mastery of Specific Skills
One of the most important factors to consider when measuring success in skills-based learning is the mastery of specific skills. Students in skills-based learning programs are typically expected to develop a specific set of skills or competencies related to their chosen industry or profession.

To measure success in this context, it is important to assess the student's mastery of these specific skills. This may involve using objective measures, such as exams, assessments, or practical evaluations, to determine whether the student has achieved a certain level of proficiency in the targeted skills.

Application of Skills in Real-World Settings
Measuring success in skills-based learning also requires assessing the student's ability to apply their skills in real-world settings. While mastery of specific skills is important, it is equally important to ensure that students are able to use these skills in practical situations.

To measure success in this context, it may be useful to observe the student's performance in a real-world setting, such as during an internship or work placement. Alternatively, it may be possible to use simulations or case studies to assess the student's ability to apply their skills in practical situations.

Engagement and Motivation
Engagement and motivation are also important factors to consider when measuring success in skills-based learning. Students who are engaged and motivated are more likely to succeed in their program and to continue to develop their skills and knowledge over time.

To measure success in this context, it may be useful to assess the student's level of engagement and motivation throughout their program. This may involve using surveys or other assessment tools to gather feedback from the student and to determine whether they are actively engaged in their learning.

Collaboration and Teamwork
Collaboration and teamwork are important skills for success in many industries and professions. Students in skills-based learning programs are often required to work in teams or collaborate with others in order to complete projects or assignments.

To measure success in this context, it may be useful to assess the student's ability to collaborate and work effectively in a team. This may involve observing the student's performance in group projects or assignments or using self-assessment tools to gather feedback from the student and their peers.

Professionalism and Work Ethic

Professionalism and work ethic are also important factors to consider when measuring success in skills-based learning. Students in skills-based learning programs are typically expected to behave in a professional manner and to adhere to high standards of ethics and conduct. To measure success in this context, it may be useful to assess the student's level of professionalism and work ethic throughout their program. This may involve using objective measures, such as assessments of the student's adherence to professional standards and ethics, or using self-assessment tools to gather feedback from the student and their peers on their work habits and attitudes.

Progress Over Time

Measuring progress over time is another important factor to consider when measuring success in skills-based learning. Students may not demonstrate mastery of a skill or competency immediately but may show progress over time as they continue to develop their skills. It is important to measure the student's progress over time to ensure that they are making steady progress towards their goals and that they are developing their skills and knowledge in a meaningful way.

To measure progress over time, it may be useful to use assessments or evaluations at regular intervals throughout the program. This will allow educators and students to track progress over time and to make adjustments to the program or the student's learning plan as needed.

Integration of Learning Across Multiple Domains

Skills-based learning often involves learning across multiple domains, such as technical skills, interpersonal skills, and professional skills. Success in skills-based learning requires that students be able to integrate their learning across these multiple domains and to apply their skills in a holistic and meaningful way. To measure success in this context, it may be useful to assess the student's ability to integrate their learning across multiple domains. This may involve using assessments or evaluations that require the student to demonstrate their skills and knowledge in a real-world context that integrates multiple domains.

Use Multiple Measures
Measuring success in skills-based learning requires using multiple measures to ensure that a comprehensive picture of the student's progress and achievements is obtained. This may involve using a combination of objective measures, such as exams and assessments, as well as more subjective measures, such as feedback from the student and their peers.

Align Measures With Learning Objectives
It is important to align measures with the learning objectives of the program or course. This will ensure that the measures are directly related to the skills and competencies that students are expected to develop in the program.

Use a Rubric or Scoring Guide
Using a rubric or scoring guide can help ensure consistency in the assessment of student performance. This will help to ensure that all students are evaluated in a fair and objective manner and that the measures are reliable and valid.

Provide Feedback to Students
Providing feedback to students is an important part of measuring success in skills-based learning. Feedback can help students understand their strengths and weaknesses, identify areas for improvement, and make adjustments to their learning plan.

Involve Students in the Assessment Process
Involving students in the assessment process can help to increase their engagement and motivation as well as provide them with a greater sense of ownership and control over their learning. This may involve using self-assessment tools or involving students in the development of assessment measures.

Measuring success in skills-based learning can be a complex and challenging task, but it is essential for ensuring that students are developing the skills and competencies they need to succeed in their chosen industry or profession. By considering factors such as mastery of specific skills, application of skills in real-world settings, engagement and motivation, collaboration and teamwork, professionalism and work ethic, progress over time, and integration of learning across multiple domains, educators and administrators can develop effective strategies for measuring success in skills-based learning. By using multiple measures, aligning measures with learning objectives, using rubrics or scoring guides, providing feedback to students, and involving students in the assessment process, educators and administrators can ensure that measures are reliable, valid, and fair and that students are receiving the feedback and support they need to succeed.

14

Assessment

I'll be honest; whenever I get a record of assessment from another educator, I take it in but really like to come to my own conclusions. These are people we're working with, and everyone is constantly growing, expanding, and changing. I don't think it's the best practice to use an assessment that may be years old as a gauge of where a person is now. I once had a student come to us, and, in his behavioral plan, it said he was "line of sight, 100% of the time." Usually, that means there are behaviors that can lead to injury or difficulty to themselves or those around them. Upon arrival, I couldn't disagree more. When implementing all of what we've talked about so far, I was expecting him to behave in a completely different manner. He ended up volunteering to help clean up, wanted to stay after to keep learning, and expressed to us he felt "home."

Training vs Educational Assessments

As mentioned earlier, assessments in a training environment and an educational setting are similar in that they both aim to measure an individual's knowledge and skills. However, there are some key differences between the two that are worth exploring in more detail.

In a training environment, assessment is typically focused on determining whether an individual has the knowledge and skills necessary to perform a specific job or task. This is often done through the use of practice tests, such as simulations or on-the-job evaluations, which measure an individual's ability to apply their knowledge and skills in a real-world setting. For example, a construction company might assess the skills of its workers by having them complete a task such as building a small structure, or a software company might assess the skills of its developers by having them complete a coding challenge. The focus of these assessments is to ensure that employees are equipped to perform their job responsibilities effectively and efficiently.

In contrast, assessment in an educational setting is typically focused on measuring an individual's understanding of a subject or material. This is often done through the use of tests, quizzes, and essays, which measure an individual's knowledge and comprehension of the material. These assessments are typically given at regular intervals throughout the educational program, such as at the end of a semester or course, and are used to evaluate student learning and progress. The focus of these assessments is to determine the level of understanding and mastery that students have attained.

One of the main differences between the two is that training assessments are often more objective, while educational assessments are often more subjective. This is because training assessments are focused on determining whether an individual has the necessary knowledge and skills to perform a specific task, and these skills can be measured quantitatively. For example, an individual's ability to use a specific software application or to read a blueprint can be objectively measured by the number of errors made or by the speed at which the task is completed. Educational assessments, on the other hand, are focused on determining an individual's understanding and comprehension of a subject or material, which is often more difficult to measure quantitatively. For example, an individual's understanding of a historical event or a literary work can be difficult to quantify. Therefore, these types of assessments rely more on subjective measures such as essays or open-ended questions.

Another key difference between the two is that training assessments are often used to measure an individual's progress over time, while educational assessments are typically used to measure an individual's knowledge and understanding at a specific point in time. For example, a construction worker might be assessed on their ability to use a specific tool at the beginning of their training and then again after a few months on the job to measure their progress. In contrast, a student might be assessed on their understanding of a historical event at the end of a semester or course. This difference in the timing of assessments reflects the different goals of the two types of assessments. Training assessments are used to ensure that employees are developing the necessary skills and knowledge to perform their job responsibilities effectively and efficiently, while educational assessments are used to evaluate student learning and progress.

It's important to note that both assessment types have their own benefits and limitations. Training assessments are useful for ensuring that employees have the necessary knowledge and skills to perform their job responsibilities effectively and efficiently. They provide employers with a clear understanding of the strengths and weaknesses of their employees, which can be used to guide training and development programs. However, training assessments can be time-consuming and costly to administer, and they may not take into account the unique circumstances and challenges that employees may face on the job.

Educational assessments, on the other hand, provide employees with feedback on their learning and progress, and they help employers to identify areas where they may need additional support. However, these assessments may not address the challenges that employees may face on the job. Additionally, training assessments may not fully capture the complexity of certain job tasks, and may not account for the ability of employees to adapt and learn on the job.

On the other hand, educational assessments are useful for evaluating student learning and progress in an educational setting. They provide teachers and educators with valuable information about student understanding and comprehension of a subject or material, which can be used to guide instruction and curriculum development. However, educational assessments can also have limitations. They may not fully capture the complexity of certain subjects or the unique learning styles and abilities of students. Additionally, educational assessments may be prone to bias and may not take into account the various factors that can impact student performance, such as socioeconomic status or language barriers.

Assessments in a training environment and an educational setting are similar in that they both aim to measure an individual's knowledge and skills, but they are different in their focus and methods. Training assessments are focused on determining an individual's ability to perform a specific task, while educational assessments are focused on determining an individual's understanding and comprehension of a subject or material. Both types of assessment have their own benefits and limitations, and it is important to consider the specific goals and context of the assessment when choosing an appropriate assessment method. It is important to use a combination of both assessment types to have a more holistic view of the individuals in question, whether they are employees or students.

15
Feedback

Feedback is an essential aspect of any workplace, and it plays a critical role in the development and performance of employees. Clear, kind, honest, and encouraging feedback can help employees understand their strengths and areas for improvement, and can also help them feel more engaged and motivated in their work.

Provide feedback in a clear and specific manner rather than being vague or overly critical. Use nonjudgmental language, and avoiding language that may be perceived as negative or dismissive. Be mindful of the individual's learning style, and adapt the feedback to suit their needs. Be open to the individual's perspective, and take their input into account when providing feedback. Provide feedback in a timely manner rather than waiting until a significant amount of time has passed.

Provide both positive and constructive feedback, and highlight strengths as well as areas for improvement. Avoid overloading the individual with feedback and instead provide feedback in small, manageable chunks. Be aware of the cultural, social, and linguistic diversity of the individual, and provide feedback accordingly.

Be aware of the individual's emotional state while providing feedback, and encourage self-reflection, providing opportunities for the individual to reflect on their own performance and progress.

Clear feedback refers to providing specific and actionable information to employees. It should be easy to understand and directly related to the employee's role and responsibilities. This type of feedback helps employees understand what they are doing well and what they need to improve on. Clear feedback also helps employees to set specific goals and understand their progress towards those goals. For example, instead of saying, "You need to improve your customer service skills," it would be more helpful to say, "When interacting with customers, try to use active listening and rephrase their concerns to make sure you understand them before addressing them."

Kind feedback is about providing feedback in a respectful and professional manner. It should be constructive and not personal, focusing on the behavior and not the person. Kind feedback is also delivered with empathy and understanding, avoiding judgment or criticism. It is important to remember that every employee has different strengths and weaknesses, and a kind approach can help them to overcome their weaknesses and develop their strengths. Additionally, kind feedback can help to create a positive work environment where employees feel valued and respected, which can lead to a more productive and motivated workforce.

Honest feedback is about being truthful and transparent with employees. It is important to be honest with employees about their performance, both good and bad. Honest feedback helps employees understand their performance in an objective and accurate way and can also help them to identify areas for improvement. It is important for employers to provide honest feedback in a timely manner so that employees can take steps to improve their performance. Providing honest feedback also helps to create a culture of trust and transparency in the workplace.

Encouraging feedback is about providing positive reinforcement and highlighting the achievements of employees. It helps to build employee confidence, motivation, and engagement. Encouraging feedback also helps employees to understand their value to the organization, and it can be a great tool for recognizing and rewarding good performance. Encouraging feedback can also help to create a positive work environment where employees feel motivated and engaged in their work.

Providing clear, kind, honest, and encouraging feedback is a continuous process; it's not just a one-time event but should be integrated into the regular interactions between the employer and the employee. Regular feedback helps to keep employees informed about their performance and progress, and it can also help to identify any potential issues early on. Additionally, providing regular feedback can help to create a culture of continuous improvement and development, where employees feel that they are constantly growing and learning in their roles.

It is also important for employers to consider the timing of feedback; it should be provided in a timely manner, not too soon or too late. Feedback should be given when the event or behavior occurs; this way, it is still fresh in the employee's mind, and they can make the necessary changes. Additionally, when feedback is given in a timely manner, it can help to prevent small issues from becoming bigger problems.

Clear, kind, honest, and encouraging feedback is essential for the development and performance of employees. It helps employees understand their strengths and areas for improvement and can also help them to feel more engaged and motivated in their work. Employers should strive to provide clear, kind, honest, and encouraging feedback in a timely and respectful manner and should make it a regular part of their interactions with employees. By doing so, they can foster a positive and productive work environment where employees feel safe and successful.

3
Placement

16
Portfolio

Often, when we think of adults getting placed into careers, we think of the stories we see on TV and the fairytales where everything works out perfectly in the end. The stories that are told go something like this:

Once there was a young adult named Jack, who was diagnosed with autism at a young age. Growing up, Jack had a hard time making friends and communicating with others, and he found it difficult to understand social cues and emotions. He also struggled with certain academic subjects, such as math and science, but he had always been fascinated with technology and electronics.

Despite his difficulties, Jack was determined to succeed. He graduated high school and decided to attend a community college to study computer science. It was a difficult transition for him, as he struggled to keep up with the fast-paced curriculum and the social aspect of college life. But he was determined to overcome these barriers, and he worked hard to improve his communication and social skills.

After completing his associate degree, Jack transferred to a four-year university to study computer engineering. It was a challenging experience, but he was able to adapt to the new environment and excel in his coursework. He found that he was able to understand complex technical concepts with ease, and he was able to communicate effectively with his professors and classmates.

Upon graduation, Jack faced another barrier – finding a job. He knew that it would be difficult for him to find a job in his field, as employers were often hesitant to hire individuals with autism. But he was determined to pursue his passion, and he spent months sending out resumes and attending job fairs.

Finally, Jack landed an interview at a tech company that specialized in developing assistive technology for individuals with disabilities. He was a little nervous, but he tried his best to be friendly and professional. He answered the questions about his work experience and skills, and he also talked about his passion for technology and helping others. The interviewer was impressed by his enthusiasm and willingness to learn, and they offered him the job on the spot.

Jack was overjoyed. He couldn't believe that he had found a job that he was truly interested in and that aligned with his passion to help others with disabilities. He was excited to start working and learn more about the field of assistive technology.

As he worked at the tech company, Jack began to realize that his passion for technology could be more than just a hobby. He was able to use his skills and knowledge to create innovative solutions that helped improve the lives of individuals with disabilities. He was able to overcome the barriers that he faced and found a career that he was truly passionate about. Jack was no longer just a young adult with autism; he was a successful engineer, who was respected and valued for his contributions.

Doesn't that read just like you'd expect? But the thing is, that's not how it works. The starting place for a real-life story of success is a portfolio. A portfolio is a collection of work samples that demonstrate a person's abilities and accomplishments. They are commonly used by artists, designers, and other creative professionals to showcase their work but work really well with the neurodiverse community to demonstrate their skills and experience.

There are several benefits of using a portfolio over a traditional resume:

- ♦ A portfolio allows you to showcase your work in a more dynamic and interactive way, giving potential employers a better sense of your abilities and skills.

- It allows you to present a more comprehensive view of your work, including examples of your process and problem-solving skills.
- A portfolio enables you to demonstrate your work in the context of real-world projects, which can be more meaningful to potential employers than a list of job duties and responsibilities.
- It allows you to highlight your strengths and achievements in a way that a traditional resume cannot.
- Portfolios can be updated regularly, keeping your work current and relevant.
- It allows you to present your work in a more visual way, making it more engaging and easier to understand.
- A portfolio can provide context for your experience, allowing potential employers to understand the impact of your work on specific projects or initiatives.
- It allows you to personalize your presentation, giving potential employers a better sense of who you are as a person and professional.
- It can also help you stand out in a crowded job market, as many job applicants submit only a traditional resume.
- A portfolio can also be an effective tool for networking and building professional relationships, as it allows you to share your work with others and get feedback.

A portfolio can include a wide range of materials, such as written work, design samples, photographs, videos, and other forms of creative or professional output. It can also include information about educational background, professional development, and certifications. It can also include examples of previous projects you've worked on, testimonials from clients or colleagues, and any awards you've received.

Creating a Portfolio

Creating a portfolio can be a useful way to stand out in a crowded job market, and it can be beneficial for individuals in any field.

For example, a welder or carpenter might include a selection of their designs in their portfolio, while a software developer might include code samples. It can also be a useful tool for entrepreneurs to showcase their work to potential clients.

When creating a portfolio, it is important to keep in mind the audience and the purpose of the portfolio – to attain a career – not just a job. The portfolio should be tailored to the specific industry or job the person is applying for and should highlight the most relevant and impressive work they have done. It's important to be selective about what you include in your portfolio and focus on the most impressive and relevant pieces of work.

The portfolio should also be organized in a clear and user-friendly way with a clear introduction and easy navigation. It should be visually appealing and easy to read. This can include using a clean and simple design, clear headings and subheadings, and high-quality images or videos. In addition to a traditional portfolio, there are also digital portfolio platforms that allow individuals to create an online portfolio that can be shared with potential employers or clients. These digital portfolios can include interactive elements, such as videos, audio recordings, and animations, and can easily be updated and shared with others. This can be a great way to make your portfolio easily accessible to potential employers or employment opportunities and to keep it up to date with your latest work.

When it comes to the actual content of the portfolio, it's important to be honest and accurate about your skills and experience. But you should also be strategic in the way you present your information. For example, if you're applying for a job as a copywriter, you might want to include examples of your writing skills in the form of blog posts, articles, or advertising copy. But if you're applying for a job as a project manager, you might want to focus more on examples of your leadership and organizational skills.

Another important aspect of a portfolio is to include any personal projects you have worked on; this can give an insight to the employer about your passion, creativity, and hardworking attitude. Personal projects can include anything from a side business you started to a volunteer project you led to an art piece you created. Employers often see personal projects as evidence of your ambition, resourcefulness, and problem-solving skills.

It's also important to keep in mind that your portfolio will likely be one of many that an employer or client sees, so it's important to make it as memorable and distinctive as possible. This can include incorporating your own personal style or brand into the portfolio or including a unique element that sets it apart from others.

Presenting a Portfolio

Preparation and presenting your portfolio during a job interview is a crucial step towards securing your dream job. At TACT, we do this side by side with our employment director and employment specialists. I highly recommend that during the process for our neurodivergent community and autistic individuals. The portfolio provides the candidate with the opportunity to showcase their skills, accomplishments, and expertise to the hiring manager. A portfolio is a collection of their work samples that demonstrates their skills and abilities in a particular field. It includes various documents, such as design projects, writing samples, photographs, and case studies, that illustrate your capabilities.

Research the Company and the Position

Before presenting your portfolio during a job interview, it is essential to research the company and the position you are applying for. Understand the company's mission, vision, and values, and get a clear idea of the role and responsibilities of the position. This information will help you tailor your portfolio to the company's needs and demonstrate how your skills and experience align with their requirements.

Choose Your Best Work Samples

When selecting the work samples for your portfolio, choose your best and most relevant pieces. Pick projects that highlight your strengths and showcase your versatility in your field. Be sure to include a mix of work that demonstrates your technical and creative abilities. Additionally, ensure that your work samples are recent and reflect the latest industry standards.

Organize Your Portfolio

Once you have selected your work samples, organize them in a way that is easy to navigate and visually appealing. You can arrange your work chronologically or thematically. For instance, you could group your projects by type, industry, or client. Use a consistent format and layout throughout your portfolio to create a cohesive and professional look.

Create an Introduction

Include an introduction in your portfolio that provides a brief overview of your skills, experience, and achievements. This introduction should set the tone for the rest of the portfolio and grab the interviewer's attention. Keep it concise and engaging, and ensure that it highlights your strengths and unique selling points.

Provide Context for Your Work

When presenting your work samples, provide context for each project. Explain the problem you were trying to solve, the goals you set, and the process you followed to achieve them. Also, highlight the challenges you faced and how you overcame them. This information will help the interviewer understand your thought process and approach to problem-solving.

Highlight Your Accomplishments

As you present your work, highlight your accomplishments and the results you achieved. Use metrics and data to quantify your success, such as the number of views, engagement rates, or revenue generated. Emphasize the impact of your work and how it helped the company or the client achieve their goals.

Demonstrate Your Soft Skills

In addition to showcasing your technical skills, use your portfolio to demonstrate your soft skills. Soft skills refer to personal attributes such as communication, collaboration, problem-solving, and time management. Highlight examples of how you demonstrated these skills in your projects, such as how you worked effectively with a team or communicated complex ideas to nontechnical stakeholders.

Practice Your Presentation

Practice presenting your portfolio before the job interview to ensure that you are comfortable and confident with the material. Time yourself, and make sure that you can present your work samples within the allotted time. Also, rehearse your introduction and the key points you want to highlight. Ask a friend or a mentor to provide feedback on your presentation style and content.

Bring Hard Copies of Your Portfolio

Although many companies may ask for a digital portfolio, it is always a good idea to bring hard copies of your portfolio to the job interview. These copies can be useful if the interviewer wants to refer back to your work samples or if there are technical difficulties with the digital presentation. Make sure that your hard copies are professional-looking and high-quality.

Be prepared for any questions or feedback the interviewer may have. Prepare yourself to answer questions about your work samples, your process, and your achievements. Be ready to explain why you made certain decisions and how your work aligns with the company's goals. Additionally, be open to feedback and suggestions from the interviewer. Use this opportunity to learn and grow as a professional.

Overall, a portfolio is a powerful tool that can help job seekers and professionals stand out in a crowded job market – a market that normally leaves those with autism unemployed and overlooked – and can be used to showcase their work and qualifications in a way that a traditional resume cannot. Most importantly, it helps autistic individuals truly showcase their work and talent and by creating well-organized, visually appealing content. While there is still value to a resume, portfolios really work well for the autism community's ability and put their talent and skill on full display so that someone can view them objectively.

17
Work-Based Interview

The traditional interview process, in which a candidate is asked a set of predetermined questions, has long been the standard method for evaluating job applicants. But it's not a way to operate in the best interest of the neurodiverse community, nor should our community be asked to mask and conform. But it will happen and does happen. This method has its limitations, and a new approach has emerged in recent years: the work-based interview. Work-based interviews are designed to assess a candidate's skills, knowledge, and abilities in a real-world setting rather than relying solely on their responses to interview questions. This approach has been shown to be a more accurate and effective way of evaluating job applicants, and it is becoming increasingly popular among employers.

The traditional interview process has a number of limitations. One of the main limitations is that it relies heavily on the candidate's ability to communicate effectively. It hits the neurodiverse community hard, and this can be a problem for some candidates, particularly those who may be introverted or anxious like an autistic individual. In addition, traditional interviews are often based on a set of predetermined questions, which can limit the interviewer's ability to get a sense of the candidate's true abilities and skills.

Work-based interviews, on the other hand, provide a more authentic assessment of a candidate's abilities. Instead of asking a set of predetermined questions, work-based interviews involve the candidate completing a task or project that is related to the job for which they are applying. This allows the interviewer to see the candidate's skills and abilities in action rather than just hearing about them.

One of the main advantages of work-based interviews is that they provide a more accurate assessment of a candidate's abilities. Seeing a candidate's skills in action allows the interviewer to get a better sense of the candidate's true abilities rather than relying solely on their responses to interview questions. This can lead to a more accurate assessment of the candidate's fit for the job.

Work-based interviews also provide a more realistic view of the candidate's ability to perform the job. Rather than relying on the candidate's responses to interview questions, work-based interviews allow the interviewer to see the candidate's abilities in action, in a real-world setting. This can give the interviewer a better sense of the candidate's ability to perform the job and can help to identify any potential issues that may arise.

Another advantage of work-based interviews is that they can provide a more enjoyable and engaging experience for both the interviewer and the candidate. Rather than simply asking questions, work-based interviews involve the candidate completing a task or project, which can be more interesting and engaging for both parties. In addition, work-based interviews can also be more cost-effective for employers. Traditional interviews often require a significant investment of time and resources, particularly if the employer is interviewing multiple candidates. Work-based interviews, on the other hand, can be completed in a shorter amount of time and with fewer resources.

Work-based interviews provide a more accurate and effective way of evaluating job applicants. They allow the interviewer to see a candidate's skills and abilities in action, in a real-world setting, rather than relying solely on their responses to interview questions. This approach can lead to a more accurate assessment of the candidate's fit for the job, and it can provide a more enjoyable and engaging experience for both the interviewer and the candidate. As a result, work-based interviews are becoming increasingly popular among employers as a more effective way to evaluate job applicants. Additionally, work-based interviews can also provide a more diverse and inclusive hiring process, as it allows employers to evaluate candidates based on their abilities rather than on their traditional interview skills or background. Work-based interviews can also provide an opportunity for candidates from underrepresented groups or those who may have faced barriers in their career to showcase their abilities and skills in a real-world setting.

Moreover, work-based interviews can be more beneficial for the employer as well as the employee. This can result in a more productive and efficient workforce as the new hires are more likely to possess the skills and abilities required for the job.

On the other hand, work-based interviews can also be beneficial for the employee. The opportunity to showcase their skills and abilities in practice can lead to a better job match and a more satisfying career for the employee.

However, it's important to note that work-based interviews aren't always the best approach for every job or every candidate. Certain jobs, such as those in customer service or sales, may require traditional interview skills such as communication and presentation abilities. In these cases, a traditional interview may be more appropriate. Additionally, some candidates may have difficulty completing a work-based interview due to a disability or other reason; in this case, accommodations should be made to ensure that the candidate is not at a disadvantage.

Benefits of Apprenticeship as a Work-Based Interview

As of late, one of the avenues we've been exploring at TACT is apprenticeship. Apprenticeship is a work-based training program that combines on-the-job training with classroom learning. Apprenticeships are a valuable tool for both employers and employees. They provide employees with the opportunity to gain valuable skills and experience while working, and they provide employers with a skilled and motivated workforce. In this chapter, we will explore the benefits of apprenticeship as a work-based interview for employers.

Skilled and Motivated Workforce

One of the key benefits of apprenticeship for employers is that it provides them with a skilled and motivated workforce. Apprentices are eager to learn and are motivated to succeed in their chosen field. As apprentices gain more experience, they become more valuable to the company and are better able to contribute to the success of the business.

Cost-Effective Training

Apprenticeship is a cost-effective way for employers to train their workforce. Apprenticeships are typically funded by the government, which means that employers do not have to pay for the training themselves. This can save businesses a significant amount of money, especially when compared to the cost of hiring and training new employees.

Reduced Staff Turnover

Another benefit of apprenticeship for employers is that it can help to reduce staff turnover. When employers invest in their employees and provide them with opportunities for training and career development, employees are more likely to stay with the company long-term. This can save businesses money on recruitment and training costs as well as preventing a loss of productivity that often comes with staff turnover.

Increased Productivity

Apprenticeship can also help to increase productivity within a business. As apprentices gain more experience and skills, they become more efficient at their job. This can lead to a higher level of output and better-quality work, which can ultimately help the business to be more successful.

Better Workplace Culture

Apprenticeship can also help to create a positive workplace culture. When employers invest in their employees and provide them with opportunities for training and development, it shows that they value their employees. This can lead to a more engaged and motivated workforce, which can ultimately help to create a more positive and productive workplace culture.

Real-Life Experience
One of the key benefits of apprenticeship as a work-based interview is that it provides employers with a way to assess potential employees in a real-life setting. When employers conduct interviews, they are often limited to asking questions and reviewing resumes. With apprenticeship, employers are able to see how potential employees work in a real-life setting, which can help them to make more informed hiring decisions.

Improved Fit
Another benefit of apprenticeship as a work-based interview is that it can help to ensure that new hires are a good fit for the company. When employers hire new employees, it can be difficult to determine how they will fit into the company culture and work environment. With apprenticeship, employers are able to see how potential employees work within the company culture and can make more informed hiring decisions.

Reduced Risk
Apprenticeship as a work-based interview can also help to reduce the risk associated with hiring new employees. When employers hire new employees, there is always a risk that they will not be a good fit for the company or will not perform well in their job. With apprenticeship, employers are able to see how potential employees work in a real-life setting, which can help to reduce the risk associated with hiring new employees.

Increased Retention
Apprenticeship as a work-based interview can also help to increase employee retention. When employees are given the opportunity to gain valuable skills and experience through apprenticeship, they are more likely to stay with the company long-term. This can help to reduce the costs associated with staff turnover.

Enhanced Training and Development

Apprenticeship as a work-based interview can also provide enhanced training and development opportunities for potential employees. During the apprenticeship period, employees receive on-the-job training and classroom learning, which can help to enhance their skills and knowledge. This can ultimately benefit the employer, as they will have a more skilled and knowledgeable workforce.

Improved Employee Engagement

Apprenticeship as a work-based interview can also help to improve employee engagement. When potential employees are given the opportunity to participate in an apprenticeship program, it shows that the employer is invested in their success. This can help to create a sense of loyalty and engagement among employees, which can ultimately lead to a more productive and motivated workforce.

Competitive Advantage

Finally, apprenticeship as a work-based interview can provide employers with a competitive advantage. When employers invest in their employees and provide them with opportunities for training and development, they are more likely to attract and retain top talent. This can ultimately help the business to be more successful, as they will have a skilled and motivated workforce.

Apprenticeship as a work-based interview can provide a range of benefits for employers. It can help to create a skilled and motivated workforce, reduce staff turnover, increase productivity, improve workplace culture, provide real-life experience, improve fit, reduce risk, increase retention, provide enhanced training and development, improve employee engagement, and provide a competitive advantage. By investing in their employees through apprenticeship, employers can create a more successful and sustainable business. It is important for employers to recognize the value of apprenticeship and to incorporate it into their recruitment and training strategies.

18

Talent Over Charity

TACT has won three different car shows it's entered. These aren't the run-of-the-mill small auto enthusiast meet-ups in a food store parking lot. These are big shows with lots of amazing cars and talented auto enthusiasts. At each show, we did not advertise that our cars were restored by autistic individuals. Why? Because we want the talent to be upfront. And in each instance, we won. Then, the measurement of talent is objective, not subjective.

Hiring based on talent rather than charity is crucial for businesses in order to ensure their success. When a company hires an employee based on their qualifications and skills, they are investing in someone who can help the company achieve its goals and objectives. On the other hand, hiring based on charity can lead to a lack of productivity and can hinder the company's progress.

One of the main reasons businesses should hire based on talent over charity is that it can lead to increased productivity. Autistic individuals have a lot to offer! The *Harvard Business Review* did a study and found that, when compared to a neurotypical employee, a neurodiverse employee was 140% more productive – that's just good business! When an employee is hired based on their qualifications and skills, they are more likely to have the necessary knowledge and experience to perform their job effectively. This can lead to faster and more efficient completion of tasks, which can ultimately help the company achieve its goals.

Another benefit of hiring based on talent is that it can lead to a more motivated workforce. When employees are hired based on their qualifications and skills, they are more likely to be engaged and motivated in their work. This can lead to higher job satisfaction and a more positive work environment.

Furthermore, hiring based on talent can also help to reduce turnover rates. When employees are hired based on their qualifications and skills, they are more likely to be a good fit for the company and are less likely to be looking for other job opportunities. This can help to reduce the costs associated with employee turnover and can help to ensure that the company has a stable workforce.

Additionally, hiring based on talent can also help businesses to attract and retain top talent. Inclusivity draws in better talent. When a company is known for hiring employees based on their qualifications and skills, it can attract other highly qualified and skilled individuals who are looking for a challenging and rewarding career.

However, it's also important to consider that businesses should be socially responsible and consider diversity and inclusivity when hiring. By having a diverse and inclusive workforce, companies can benefit from different perspectives and ideas, which can lead to more innovative solutions and a more inclusive work environment.

Hiring based on talent rather than charity is crucial for businesses to be successful. It can lead to increased productivity, a more motivated workforce, reduced turnover rates, and the ability to attract and retain top talent while also considering diversity and inclusivity in the hiring process.

19
Employer Communication

Effective communication is a crucial aspect of any workplace, and it is especially important for employers to effectively communicate with their employees. Employer communication to employees can take many forms, such as formal meetings, informal conversations, and written communication. The goal of effective employer communication is to ensure that employees are informed, motivated, and engaged in their work.

One of the most common forms of employer communication is through regular meetings. These meetings can be held on a daily, weekly, or monthly basis and can be used to discuss important issues, provide updates on company progress, and address any concerns that employees may have. In all these cases, the information must be presented at least 24 hours in advance and in multiple ways. It is important for employers to ensure that these meetings are well organized, productive, and inclusive with ample time allocated for employee input and feedback. Employers should also make sure that the agenda of the meeting is communicated in advance and that the meeting is run efficiently and effectively. Meetings should be followed by a summary of the main points discussed and any action items that need to be taken.

Informal communication is also an important aspect of employer–employee communication. This can include casual conversations, emails, or text messages and can be used to address more specific or immediate concerns as well as to build positive relationships with employees. Employers should strive to foster a culture of open communication where employees feel comfortable approaching them with any issues or concerns they may have. They should also be responsive and timely in addressing any concerns raised by employees. This can help to build trust and loyalty among employees and create a more positive work environment.

Written communication is another essential aspect of employer communication. This includes written policies, procedures, and guidelines as well as emails and other forms of written correspondence. Written communication is a useful tool for providing clear and consistent information to employees and can be used to communicate important information, such as changes to company policies or updates on company performance. Employers should also ensure that all written communication is clear and easy to understand. They should use simple language and avoid using jargon or technical terms that employees may not understand.

It is also important for employers to be aware of the different communication styles and preferences of their employees. Some employees may prefer face-to-face communication, while others may prefer written or electronic communication. Employers should strive to accommodate the communication preferences of their employees in order to ensure that they are effectively communicating with all employees. This can be done through a variety of methods such as surveying employees, conducting one-on-one meetings, or providing different communication channels for employees to choose from.

Another important aspect of employer communication is providing employees with regular feedback on their performance. This can include both positive and constructive feedback and should be provided in a timely and respectful manner. Regular feedback can help employees understand their strengths and areas for improvement and can also help them feel more engaged in their work. Feedback should be provided in a manner that is specific, actionable, and relevant to the employee's role and responsibilities. Employers should also ensure that feedback is provided in a confidential manner and that employees feel comfortable discussing their performance with their managers.

Effective employer communication can also help to build trust and loyalty among employees. When employees feel that their opinions and concerns are valued and respected, they are more likely to be motivated and engaged in their work, which can lead to better performance, productivity, and overall satisfaction. Employers should also ensure that communication is consistent and transparent; this can help to build trust and credibility among employees.

Another important aspect of employer communication is the use of technology. In today's digital age, technology has become an important tool for communication, and employers should take advantage of this. For example, employers can use video to help prepare for meetings and training. We live in an age where so many people use YouTube. It's a tool people are familiar with and comfortable with – embrace it!

20
Assimilation vs Integration

Assimilation and integration are important concepts to understand, especially when diving into the history of how the neurodiverse community has been treated in the past and especially as it pertains to individuals with autism. The history isn't great, and there are a lot of barriers to overcome.

Assimilation, in the traditional sense, refers to the process by which a minority group adopts the customs, values, and norms of the "dominant" or, in this case, the neurotypical culture and individual. In the case of the neurodivergent community, this is often called "masking" to assimilate. Assimilation can be seen as a one-way process where the neurodiverse group is expected to conform to the neurotypical culture without any reciprocal changes to the neurotypical culture. This can lead to the erasure of cultural identity and a sense of alienation from one's own community.

Integration and inclusivity, on the other hand, refer to the process of bringing different groups together in a society while allowing them to maintain their cultural identities. It emphasizes the idea of equal participation in society and mutual respect for all people. This can be seen as a two-way process where the neurodiverse group or autistic individual is accepted and respected for their unique way of thinking, understanding, and processing while also being encouraged to be their authentic self rather than masking and to be present fully in the larger society.

It's important to note that these concepts can be difficult to separate in practice for some and are often embraced as a "program" rather than a culture of inclusivity. Furthermore, integration and inclusivity can be a complex and multidimensional process that involves different dimensions such as economic, social, cultural, political, and legal integration, so setting it up can be difficult in the wrong setting. Economic integration refers to the ability of minority groups – like the neurodiverse community – to access equal economic opportunities, social integration refers to the ability of minority groups to access equal social opportunities, cultural integration refers to the ability of minority groups to access equal cultural opportunities, political integration refers to the ability of minority groups to access equal political opportunities, and legal integration refers to the ability of minority groups to access equal legal opportunities.

The concept of assimilation has often been criticized for its lack of recognition of cultural diversity and its expectation that the neurodiverse community should give up their cultural identity in order to fit in with neurotypicals. This can lead to a sense of alienation and marginalization in our community. On the other hand, integration is a more inclusive concept that values cultural diversity and promotes mutual understanding and respect between different groups.

There are so many laws and regulations that make it harder for individuals with autism to find and retain gainful employment and have full advancement throughout the length of a career. These policies have had lasting negative impacts on all communities and have only recently been acknowledged and addressed through the process of acceptance and inclusion.

Often, the "ah-ha" moment comes for people when they realize that, by embracing an authentic inclusive model, it's best practice for *everyone*. Studies have shown how afraid individuals are to share they're autistic or neurodiverse for fear of repercussions. For example, in 2023, it's still legal to pay individuals with autism less than minimum wage (although there was a law passed to change it) – that's how far we still have to go!

We must model inclusivity and move past the idea of assimilation. It's going to be a foundational point for successful transition into adulthood and employment.

21
Job Coaching

Job coaching for neurodiverse employees in the workplace is a process that involves helping individuals with neurological conditions such as autism, ADHD, and dyslexia to develop the skills and strategies they need to succeed in their jobs. Twenty percent of the population is neurodiverse, and 5.4 million adults have autism. Job coaching may include providing training on specific tasks, teaching organizational and time-management skills, and helping employees to communicate effectively with their colleagues and supervisors.

One important aspect of job coaching for neurodiverse employees is understanding the unique strengths and challenges of each individual and tailoring the coaching process accordingly. Don't think of these as accommodations but as success enablers; an employee with ADHD or autism may benefit from frequent breaks and a structured work environment, while an employee with autism may need additional support with social interactions and understanding nonverbal cues – color coding, for example, is an amazing policy, especially with clear and well-defined task analysis.

When coaching employees with autism, it is important to remember that they may require additional support and accommodations to succeed in the workplace. Some strategies for job coaching employees with autism include:

- ♦ Providing Clear and Specific Instructions: Individuals with autism may have difficulty with abstract

concepts and may benefit from clear and specific instructions.
- Creating a Predictable Work Environment: Individuals with autism may have difficulty with change and may benefit from a predictable work environment.
- Providing Visual Aids: Visual aids such as pictures and diagrams may help employees with autism understand instructions and tasks.
- Encouraging Independence: Employees with autism may thrive when given the opportunity to work independently.

But let's be very clear; it's not on the individual with autism to mask, change, or adapt. Businesses should create a welcoming and inclusive work environment for employees with autism for their – and the business's – success. Employers can create an inclusive work environment by:

- Providing training and education to all employees about autism and how to work effectively with employees on the spectrum.
- Encouraging open communication and understanding of the unique needs of employees with autism.
- Providing accommodations such as flexible scheduling or noise-canceling headphones to support employees with autism.
- Fostering a culture of acceptance and understanding.

It's also essential to establish clear expectations and guidelines for the employee's role and to provide consistent feedback on their performance. This can help to ensure that the employee understands their responsibilities and feels motivated to succeed.

It's important to work closely with the employee's supervisor, and other members of the team, to ensure that they are aware of the employee's strengths and challenges and can provide appropriate support and accommodations. This can also help to create a more inclusive and understanding work environment for everyone.

Job coaching for neurodiverse employees is a process that requires understanding, patience, and tailoring the coaching process to specific employee strengths and challenges. Clear expectations, consistent feedback, and team support are essential to success. However, please note that the information provided here is general and should not be taken as specific advice for a particular individual or situation.

22

Parent Expectations

In our very first year at TACT, we had a student come into our "Career Tracks" program to get ready for a career. His parents told us he really loved computer science, and that's what they wanted him to do. Just about every 45 minutes in our program, he had a seizure and tried to get out of class. It clearly was not working.

Then, one day, he looked out the window into the garage and saw a carpentry class we had going on. Our teachers took him out there, and he just lit up. We ended up moving him into that class, and all of a sudden, the seizures went away, and he could focus for hours at a time. He's a completely different person in carpentry class vs the technology class. Clearly, carpentry was his passion, not his parents'. We ended up getting him a job restoring furniture, and he loves it!

I say this because parental expectations play a crucial role in shaping a child's academic and professional future. Parents' expectations for their child's education and career can have a significant impact on a child's motivation, self-esteem, and overall well-being.

Positive parental expectations can be a powerful motivator for children. When parents believe in their child's abilities and have high expectations for their academic and career success, children are more likely to strive for excellence and to achieve their goals. This can lead to increased self-esteem and confidence, which can contribute to a child's overall well-being. Research has shown that children who have high expectations for their academic and career success tend to perform better academically and have a more positive attitude toward their education.

However, it's also important for parents to have realistic expectations for their children. Unrealistic expectations can lead to disappointment and frustration for both the parent and the child. It's important for parents to understand their child's abilities and limitations and to set expectations that are in line with their child's potential. It's also important for parents to recognize that every child has their own unique strengths and weaknesses and to set expectations accordingly.

Additionally, it's important for parents to communicate their expectations clearly and to provide support and guidance to help their child achieve their goals. This can include providing the resources and opportunities needed for the child to succeed, such as access to quality education, extracurricular activities, and mentorship. It's also important for parents to have open and honest communication with their child so that they understand their expectations and can work together to achieve them.

Furthermore, parental expectations also include how they view education and career paths. Some parents may have a traditional view of education where a college degree and a traditional career is the ultimate goal. But in today's world, there are many different paths to success, and it's important for parents to recognize that there are other options such as vocational training, apprenticeships, and entrepreneurship. Parents should be open-minded and supportive of their child's chosen path, regardless of what it may be.

Parental expectations can play a powerful role in shaping an individual's academic and professional future. However, it's important for parents to have realistic expectations, to communicate their expectations clearly, and to provide support and guidance to help their child achieve their goals. It's also important for parents to be openminded about different paths to success and to support their child's interests and passions.

While parental expectations can be beneficial, it's important for parents to also consider their child's own interests and goals.

A child's personal interests and passions can play a significant role in their motivation and engagement in their education and career.

It's important for parents to take the time to understand their child's interests and passions and to support them in pursuing those interests. This can include encouraging them to participate in extracurricular activities that align with their interests or providing opportunities for them to explore different career options. By supporting their child's interests and passions, parents can help to increase their child's motivation and engagement in their education and career.

Furthermore, it's important for parents to respect their child's autonomy and to allow them to make their own decisions about their education and career. This can include giving them the freedom to choose the courses they want to take or to explore different career options. By providing support and guidance while also respecting their child's autonomy, parents can help their child to achieve their goals while also fostering independence and self-motivation.

23

Benefits

I could tell you lots of stories from organizations that have hired TACT grads and experienced the benefits firsthand. One comes to mind as of late. One of our grads – let's call her Jill – got a job working at the largest beer manufacturer in Colorado – the one that "taps the Rockies." On her first day, she noticed something that needed to change and spoke up. They listened and realized she was right. Day one! How incredible is that? Now, they're making more money because of what she noticed.

Another grad started working for a local electrical supplier. It's a really big company that services the whole state. He was so good at the job that they ended up letting go of three neurotypicals because he was doing more than all of them combined. Incredible.

But let's understand that not all individuals on the spectrum are the same. Everyone is unique and offers different benefits to employers. The term "neurodiversity" refers to the range of variations in the human brain, including those that are commonly considered to be neurological disorders such as autism, ADHD, and dyslexia. Neurodiversity encompasses a wide range of cognitive and neurological differences, including those that are considered to be disabilities. In recent years, there has been an increasing awareness and acceptance of neurodiversity in the workplace with more and more organizations recognizing the benefits of hiring neurodiverse employees.

One of the main benefits of hiring neurodiverse employees is increased diversity of thought and perspective. Neurodiverse individuals often have unique ways of thinking and problem-solving, which can lead to new and innovative solutions to problems. This can be particularly valuable in industries that require creative and out-of-the-box thinking, such as technology and design.

Another benefit of hiring neurodiverse employees is that they can bring a unique set of skills to the workplace. For example, individuals with autism may have strong attention to detail and a strong ability to focus on a task, which can be valuable in fields such as data analysis and programming. Similarly, individuals with ADHD may have strong multitasking skills, which can be beneficial in roles that require the ability to handle multiple tasks at once. Additionally, individuals with dyslexia may have strong spatial awareness and visual thinking skills, which can be valuable in fields such as design and architecture.

Hiring neurodiverse employees can also lead to increased empathy and understanding within an organization. By having a diverse workforce, organizations can create a more inclusive culture that values different perspectives and ways of thinking. This can lead to better collaboration and teamwork as well as a more positive and productive work environment for all employees. Additionally, having a diverse workforce can also lead to improved customer service as employees will be able to better understand and relate to the needs of a diverse customer base.

In addition, hiring neurodiverse employees can also lead to cost savings for the organization. Many neurodiverse individuals are highly motivated and hardworking, which can lead to increased productivity and efficiency. This can ultimately lead to cost savings for the organization in the long run. Additionally, organizations that prioritize diversity, equity, and inclusion often have a stronger reputation, which can lead to improved recruitment, retention, and employee satisfaction.

Moreover, organizations that have a diverse workforce tend to have a more positive and productive work environment. This is due to the fact that individuals from different backgrounds tend to have different perspectives and ideas, which leads to a more dynamic and innovative work environment. Additionally, having a diverse workforce can lead to improved problem-solving and decision-making, as different perspectives can lead to a more well-rounded and well-informed decision.

It's also important to note that hiring neurodiverse employees can lead to improved compliance with legal and regulatory requirements. Organizations have a legal responsibility to provide reasonable accommodations for employees with disabilities, and hiring neurodiverse employees can help organizations to meet these requirements.

In conclusion, hiring neurodiverse employees can bring a wide range of benefits to an organization. These benefits include increased diversity of thought and perspective, a unique set of skills, increased empathy and understanding within an organization, cost savings, improved reputation, positive and productive work environment, improved problem-solving and decision-making, and compliance with legal and regulatory requirements. As society becomes more aware of neurodiversity and all the strengths surrounding the autism community, the future will be fully inclusive, and the work created will be innovative, efficient, and incredible.

Conclusion/Final Thoughts

As a dad, I believe that hiring individuals with autism is not only good for business but also good for society as a whole. As mentioned, my own child, Dylan, has autism, and I have seen firsthand the unique strengths and talents that individuals with autism can bring to the workplace. I started this journey when he was very young. I've learned a lot, grown a lot, and seen the world change a lot. It's also been hard – really hard – but completely worth the ride, and I wouldn't change a thing.

I believe wholly in the benefits of hiring individuals with autism and that their unique perspectives and creative problem-solving abilities will change the world. My child has an incredible ability to think outside the box and come up with innovative solutions to problems. This kind of creativity can be invaluable in certain industries, such as technology or research, where unique approaches and solutions are needed.

I strongly believe that the benefit has a positive impact on workplace culture and employee morale. As a dad, I want my child to work in an environment where they feel welcomed, supported, and valued for their contributions. By promoting diversity and inclusion in the workplace, employers can create a sense of belonging for all employees, which can lead to increased job satisfaction and employee engagement.

Individuals with autism can also enhance teamwork and collaboration by bringing unique strengths and perspectives to a team. My child may not excel in every area, but they have strengths that can complement the strengths of their neurotypical peers. By recognizing and leveraging each team member's strengths, employers can create a more productive and effective team.

Hiring individuals with autism can also lead to increased productivity and efficiency. My child has strong attention to detail, a focus on accuracy, and a willingness to work independently.

These traits can be invaluable in certain industries, such as finance or data analysis, where accuracy and attention to detail are essential.

There are, of course, challenges to hiring individuals with autism that must be addressed. Communication differences, sensory sensitivities, and the need for clear expectations and routines are some of the challenges that individuals with autism may face in the workplace. As a dad, I appreciate employers who take these challenges seriously and work to create a supportive and inclusive work environment for all employees.

But as a dad, I believe that hiring individuals with autism is not only good for business but also good for society. By recognizing the unique talents and abilities of individuals with autism, employers can create a diverse and inclusive workforce that is enriched by the contributions of all employees. As a dad, I want my child to have the same opportunities as their neurotypical peers and be able to contribute their talents and skills to the workplace.

But all that is sad, looking at it from a business perspective and not the subjective dad view, hiring individuals with autism is a topic that has gained increasing attention in recent years as businesses recognize the unique strengths and abilities that individuals with autism can bring to the workplace. From a business perspective, there are numerous reasons why hiring individuals with autism makes good sense, including improved productivity, increased innovation, and enhanced social responsibility.

Improved Productivity

One of the key benefits of hiring individuals with autism is the potential for improved productivity. Individuals with autism often have strong focus and determination, which can lead to high levels of productivity and efficiency when given tasks that align with their strengths and interests. Additionally, individuals with autism often excel in detail-oriented tasks, such as data analysis or quality control, where their attention to detail and strong memory and recall can be valuable assets.

Moreover, companies that prioritize diversity and inclusion, including the hiring of individuals with autism, experience greater productivity and financial performance. A McKinsey & Company report found that companies in the top quartile for gender diversity were 15% more likely to have financial returns above their respective national industry medians. In addition, companies in the top quartile for racial and ethnic diversity were 35% more likely to have financial returns above their respective national industry medians.

To illustrate the potential impact of hiring individuals with autism, consider the case of SAP, a global software company that has made a commitment to hiring individuals with autism. Since launching its Autism at Work program in 2013, SAP has hired over 160 employees with autism, many of whom work in software testing and development roles. According to SAP, the program has been a success with employees with autism often outperforming their neurotypical peers in productivity and quality metrics.

Increased Innovation

Another significant benefit of hiring individuals with autism is increased innovation. Individuals with autism often have unique perspectives and insights, which can lead to creative problem-solving and innovative solutions. Additionally, individuals with autism may possess strong pattern-recognition abilities, allowing them to identify trends and patterns that others may miss.

Moreover, research has shown that diversity in the workplace leads to greater creativity and innovation. Studies have found that diverse teams are more likely to generate creative ideas and make better decisions than homogeneous teams. By hiring individuals with autism, businesses can bring diverse perspectives and experiences to their teams, leading to increased creativity and innovation.

To further illustrate the potential benefits of hiring individuals with autism for innovation, consider the case of HP, which has launched an Autism at Work program similar to SAP's.

According to HP, employees with autism have made significant contributions to the company's innovation efforts, such as developing new approaches to software testing and identifying previously undiscovered vulnerabilities in the company's products.

Enhanced Social Responsibility

Another important factor for businesses to consider is the social responsibility of hiring individuals with autism. By promoting diversity and inclusion, businesses can contribute to a more equitable and just society. This can help companies build goodwill and establish a positive reputation among consumers and employees. Moreover, businesses that prioritize social responsibility often experience greater customer loyalty and employee satisfaction. A study by Cone Communications found that 89% of consumers are likely to switch to a brand associated with a cause, given comparable price and quality. Additionally, a Glassdoor study found that 75% of employees expect their employer to take a stand on important social issues.

Promoting diversity and inclusion, including hiring individuals with autism, can also help businesses attract and retain talent. A study by Deloitte found that 80% of employees consider diversity and inclusion to be important when choosing an employer. By prioritizing diversity and inclusion, businesses can create a more attractive and inclusive work environment that attracts and retains top talent. In addition to the benefits discussed, there are other potential advantages to hiring individuals with autism that can further demonstrate the value of hiring individuals with autism. For example, companies that hire individuals with autism may be eligible for tax credits or other incentives. In the United States, the Work Opportunity Tax Credit provides employers with a tax credit for hiring individuals from certain target groups (this is not one of my favorite reasons, but a lot of businesses think this way), including individuals with disabilities such as autism. Similarly, in the United Kingdom, employers can receive a Disability Confident Employer accreditation, which provides recognition and support for companies that hire and retain individuals with disabilities.

Moreover, by hiring individuals with autism, businesses can help promote greater understanding and acceptance of neurodiversity in the workplace and society as a whole. This can help to break down stereotypes and reduce discrimination against individuals with autism and other neurological differences.

To maximize the benefits of hiring individuals with autism, it is important for businesses to create a supportive and inclusive work environment. This may include providing accommodations and support services, such as sensory-friendly workspaces, flexible schedules, and training and mentoring programs. Additionally, businesses can work with advocacy organizations and community groups to build relationships and better understand the needs of individuals with autism.

Hiring individuals with autism makes good business sense for a variety of reasons. From improved productivity and increased innovation to enhanced social responsibility and potential tax incentives, businesses can benefit in many ways by prioritizing diversity and inclusion in their hiring practices. By creating a supportive and inclusive work environment, businesses can help individuals with autism thrive and contribute to their full potential while also promoting a more equitable and just society. As more businesses recognize the value of hiring individuals with autism, we can move towards a more inclusive and diverse workforce that benefits us all.

Thank you again for reading. Gratitude is something I practice, and if you made it this far in my book, you may have witnessed how my mind wonders and wanders. As you read my thoughts, experiences, and ideas, I sincerely hope you see the future for the neurodiverse community as bright, full of promise for individuals, businesses, and the community. This book is a launchpad to get you thinking. I hope it does just that. The world needs the incredible strengths and talents of the autistic mind, and, as it evolves and changes, I hope it's the world that changes and not the individuals. The future is bright!

Bibliography

Bacon, Richard. "Why I Quite Like My ADHD." *BBC News*, www.bbc.com/news/uk-england-nottinghamshire-63174276

Blakeman, Adam. "More Support Needed for Neurodiverse Young People in Education and Youth Offending, Research Finds." *Keele University*, 29 July 2022, www.keele.ac.uk/about/news/2022/july/keele-research/keele-research-neurodivergent.php

Booth, Meredith. "Neurodiversity Vital to a Productive Super Industry Workforce." *Investment Magazine*, 18 May 2022, www.investment-magazine.com.au/2022/05/neurodiversity-vital-to-a-productive-super-industry-workforce

Brinbaum, Justin. "What Neurodiverse People Want Their Employers and Colleagues to Know." *Forbes*, 15 August 2022, www.forbes.com/sites/rebekahbastian/2022/08/15/what-neurodiverse-people-want-their-employers-and-colleagues-to-know

Brown, Thomas. "ADHD Is Not a Behavioral Disorder." *ADDitude*, www.additudemag.com/the-additude-interview-answer-man

CDC. "Disability and Health U.S. State Profile Data: Colorado." *Centers for Disease Control and Prevention*, 18 May 2022, www.cdc.gov/ncbddd/disabilityandhealth/impacts/colorado.html

Coan, K. E. D. "Almost 90% of Autistic Women Report Experiencing Sexual Violence, According to a New Study." *PsyPost*, 26 June 2022, www.psypost.org/2022/06/almost-90-of-autistic-women-report-experiencing-sexual-violence-according-to-a-new-study-63380

Combs, Aaron. "Opinion: We Don't Have Mental Disorders. We Have Neurodivergence. Please Use That Term Instead." *MSN*, 21 January 2023, www.msn.com/en-us/health/other/opinion-we-dont-have-mental-disorders-we-have-neurodivergence-please-use-that-term-instead/ar-AA16zMeF

Cook, Barb. "Autistic Women in the Workplace by Barb Cook, M.Aut., Dip. HSc." *NeuroEmploy Pty Ltd*, 19 January 2020, neuroemploy.com/2020/01/19/autistic-women-in-the-workplace-by-barb-cook-m-aut-dip-hsc

De Beer, Marthin. "Employees Want Financial Wellness (and It Gives Employers a Competitive Edge)." *BenefitsPRO*, www.benefitspro.com/2022/09/23/employees-want-financial-wellness-and-it-give-employers-a-competitive-edge

Diament, Michelle. "New Push Underway to Train Doctors, Dentists on Developmental Disabilities." *Disability Scoop*, 29 July 2022, www.disabilityscoop.com/2022/07/29/new-push-underway-to-train-doctors-dentists-on-developmental-disabilities/29931

Doyle, Nancy. "Neurodiversity and Innovation." *Forbes*, 9 November 2022, www.forbes.com/sites/drnancydoyle/2022/11/09/neurodiversity-and-innovation

Drake, Kimberly. "How I Support My Autistic Son to Build an Independent Life." www.medicalnewstoday.com/articles/through-my-eyes-empowering-my-son-to-negotiate-the-autism-cliff-enter-adult-life

ECMC Group. "National Study Finds High Schoolers Keenly Aware of Current in-Demand Jobs, Impacting Education Choices After Graduation." www.prnewswire.com/news-releases/national-study-finds-high-schoolers-keenly-aware-of-current-in-demand-jobs-impacting-education-choices-after-graduation-301549389.html

Edkins, Lizzie. "Why Aren't There More Video Game Characters on the Autism Spectrum?" *GamesIndustry.biz*, 15 September 2022, www.gamesindustry.biz/why-arent-there-more-video-game-characters-on-the-autism-spectrum

Elemy. "How Much ABA Therapy Costs (State by State)." *Elemy*, 28 May 2020, elemy.wpengine.com/studio/aba-therapy/costs

Ellin, Simone. "'It Can't Just Be Ford.' How Rebecca Cokley Is Centering Disability Rights at Ford and Beyond." *Inside Philanthropy*, 13 May 2022, www.insidephilanthropy.com/home/2022/5/13/it-cant-just-be-ford-how-rebecca-cokley-is-centering-disability-rights-at-ford-and-beyond

Heady, Nicola. "Why Don't Women with Autism Get Diagnosed?" *Different Brains*, 14 July 2021, differentbrains.org/why-dont-women-with-autism-get-diagnosed

Heidel, Jaime A. "Why Your Autistic Coworkers Don't Bend Rules the Way You Do." *Specialisterne USA*, 14 June 2022, www.us.specialisterne.com/why-your-autistic-coworkers-dont-bend-rules-the-way-you-do

Keane, Meghan. "How 'Unmasking' Leads to Freedom for Autistic and Other Neurodivergent People: Life Kit." *NPR*, 18 April 2022, www.

npr.org/2022/04/14/1092869514/unmasking-autism-more-inclusive-world

Konish, Lorie. "As Social Security Disability Application Wait Times Hit Record High, Experts Say It's a Sign the Agency Needs More Funding." *CNBC*, 16 September 2022, www.cnbc.com/2022/09/16/long-social-security-service-waits-signal-need-for-more-funds.html

Long, Pam. "42,000% Increase in Autism: Colorado's Invisible Epidemic." *Colorado Health Choice Alliance*, 19 November 2019, www.cohealthchoice.org/2017/12/21/42000-increase-in-autism-colorados-invisible-epidem

Mahler, Kelly, et al. "Impact of an Interoception-Based Program on Emotion Regulation in Autistic Children," 20 April 2022, https://doi.org/10.1155/2022/9328967

Martin, Charlie. "How to Prepare Teens with Autism for College?," 12 August 2022, themomkind-com.cdn.ampproject.org/c/s/themomkind.com/how-to-prepare-teens-with-autism-for-college/?amp_markup=1

Miller, Faith. "Colorado Special Education Sees Funding Increase This Year, But Is It Enough?" *Colorado Newsline*, 21 October 2021, coloradonewsline.com/2021/10/21/colorado-special-education-funding-increase

Minot, David. "7 Things Students with Disabilities Should Do When Starting College." *Autism Spectrum News*, 1 April 2022, autismspectrumnews.org/7-things-students-with-disabilities-should-do-when-starting-college

Molyneux, Vita. "New Police Jobs Ask for Neurodiverse Applicants Only." *NZ Herald*, www.nzherald.co.nz/nz/new-police-jobs-ask-for-neurodiverse-applicants-only/6FZOZWFAFNZUDIIAWMYY73MLUE

Morendo, J. Edward. "Disability Bias Should Be Addressed in AI Rules." *Advocates Say*, 6 May 2022, news.bloomberglaw.com/daily-labor-report/disability-bias-should-be-addressed-in-ai-rules-advocates-say

Oberhaus, Daniel. "Elon Musk: How Being Autistic May Make Him Think Differently," 14 November 2022, theconversation-com.cdn.ampproject.org/c/s/theconversation.com/amp/elon-musk-how-being-autistic-may-make-him-think-differently-194228

Palumbo, Jennifer "Jay." "How Autistic Individuals Can Offer Special Skills to Your Business." *Forbes*, 29 June 2022, www.forbes.com/sites/

jenniferpalumbo/2022/06/29/how-autistic-individuals-can-offer-special-skills-to-your-business

Park, Alice. "Autism Costs $2.2 Million Over a Lifetime." *Time*, 9 June 2014, time.com/2849264/the-lifetime-cost-of-autism-tops-2-million-per-person

Paul, Pamela. "The Best Extracurricular May Be an After-School Job," 30 July 2022, www.nytimes.com/2022/07/30/opinion/jobs-teenagers.html

Praslova, Ludmila. "Autism Doesn't Hold People Back at Work. Discrimination Does." *Harvard Business Review*, 13 December 2021, hbr.org/2021/12/autism-doesnt-hold-people-back-at-work-discrimination-does

Robison, John. "How Neurodiversity Has Changed." *Psychology Today*, www.psychologytoday.com/us/blog/my-life-aspergers/202208/how-neurodiversity-has-changed

Sannicandro, Tom. "Massachusetts First in the Nation to Open Colleges to Students with IDD and Autism." *Sanlaw Legal*, 28 July 2022, www.sanlaw.com/2022/07/28/massachusetts-first-in-the-nation-to-open-colleges-to-students-with-idd-and-autism

Soraghan, Tracy. "HR Magazine – Harnessing the Rich Potential of Neurodiverse Talent." *HR Magazine*, 6 February 2023, www.hrmagazine.co.uk/content/comment/harnessing-the-rich-potential-of-neurodiverse-talent

University of California. "Brain Changes in Autism Are Far More Extensive Than Previously Known." *SciTechDaily*, 5 November 2022, scitechdaily.com/brain-changes-in-autism-are-far-more-extensive-than-previously-known

Valuer, Charlotte. "Neurodiversity: Everywhere, But Hidden in the Higher Ranks." *London Business School*, 26 September 2022, www.london.edu/think/neurodiversity

Wong, Ali. "Autism Diagnosis Rates Tripled in Less Than Two Decades. What Does That Mean for Schools?," news.yahoo.com/autism-diagnosis-rates-tripled-less-100015579.html

Yehuda, Rachel. "How Parents' Trauma Leaves Biological Traces in Children." *Scientific American*, 1 July 2022, https://doi.org/10.1038/scientificamerican0722-50

Yolande, Loftus. "Autism Statistics You Need to Know in 2022." *Autism Parenting Magazine*, 28 February 2022, www.autismparentingmagazine.com/autism-statistics

Yuen, Courtney. "Club Provides Support for Neurodiverse Students at CSU." *9news.com*, 5 February 2023, www.9news.com/article/news/education/neurodiverse-students-colorado-state-university/73-8905a63b-381d-4ad9-bc2c-f82216d80f9e

Zibell, Kelsey. "4 Reasons Schools Should Prioritize Career and Technical Education." *Build Your Future*, 25 February 2020, byf.org/4-reasons-schools-should-prioritize-career-technical-education

For Product Safety Concerns and Information please contact our EU representative GPSR@taylorandfrancis.com
Taylor & Francis Verlag GmbH, Kaufingerstraße 24, 80331 München, Germany

www.ingramcontent.com/pod-product-compliance
Lightning Source LLC
Chambersburg PA
CBHW050554300426
44112CB00013B/1910